MANAGING SOFTWARE DEVELOPMENT AND MAINTENANCE

MANAGING SOFTWARE DEVELOPMENT AND MAINTENANCE

Carma L. McClure

VNR **VAN NOSTRAND REINHOLD COMPANY**
NEW YORK   CINCINNATI   ATLANTA   DALLAS   SAN FRANCISCO
           LONDON   TORONTO   MELBOURNE

Van Nostrand Reinhold Company Regional Offices:
New York   Cincinnati   Atlanta   Dallas   San Francisco

Van Nostrand Reinhold Company International Offices:
London   Toronto   Melbourne

Copyright © 1981 by Litton Educational Publishing, Inc.

Library of Congress Catalog Card Number: 80-22166
ISBN: 0-442-22569-5

All rights reserved. No part of this work covered by the copyright hereon may be reproduced or used in any form or by any means — graphic, electronic, or mechanical, including photocopying, recording, taping, or information storage and retrieval systems — without permission of the publisher.

Manufactured in the United States of America

Published by Van Nostrand Reinhold Company
135 West 50th Street, New York, N. Y. 10020

Published simultaneously in Canada by Van Nostrand Reinhold Ltd.

15 14 13 12 11 10 9 8 7 6 5 4 3 2 1

Library of Congress Cataloging in Publication Data

McClure, Carma L.
  Managing software development and maintenance.

  Bibliography: p. 197
  Includes index.
  1. Computer programming management. I. Title.
QA76.6.M28   001.64'25   80-22166
ISBN 0-442-22569-5

To My Parents

Preface

This book is intended for the software practitioner involved in the development and maintenance of software systems. It is also intended for software managers and students of software engineering. The book has been developed from a graduate course in software engineering at Illinois Institute of Technology. One of the main goals of the course is to help software engineering students become aware of the software problems in industry today.

The perspective of the book differs from that of other software engineering books in two respects. First, it focuses upon management rather than technical problems faced by the software practitioner. Second, it focuses upon software maintenance rather than software development activities.

Although recognized since the 1960s, the software crisis continues to be the bottleneck in technological advancement. While hardware costs have been dramatically decreasing, software costs are continuing to increase. Proposed solutions to software problems have concentrated on improvements in the technical aspects of software development based upon the assumption that if the quality of the software produced is improved, then software costs can be controlled. The flaw with this reasoning is that it does not also recognize the difficulty of preserving software quality as software is changed.

Change is an inherent quality of all software. Software is changed to correct errors, to improve performance, to adapt to processing environment changes and, perhaps most importantly, to accommodate changing user needs. Even a totally reliable software system that perfectly fulfills requirements is likely to be changed many times throughout its life.

Because most software has not been designed to tolerate change and because software engineers have not been taught to anticipate and to prepare for change, software quality deteriorates as a negative side-effect of change, especially during the maintenance phase.

Currently, the maintenance phase dominates the software life cycle in terms of effort and cost. In many organizations, more time is spent maintaining existing systems than developing new systems.

If software engineers and managers continue to view software as an abstract structure whose quality lies in its form rather than in its utility, software costs will continue to soar. Maintenance problems will be further compounded by the sheer number of programs to be maintained and by the increasing size and complexity of newer programs. Eventually, the maintenance effort may absorb all programming resources, leaving nothing for the development of new software.

The ultimate goal of this book, then, is to present methods to help meet the growing demands for the development and especially the maintenance of more and better quality software.

Management controls are suggested to provide for better software visibility, for a better system of checks and balances, and for better communications between the user and the software technician. The management philosophy suggested is not reactionary, of the "firefighting" sort that is so typical of many software efforts. Decisions to build or change software are not based upon a response to user pressure or a technician's desire to try the newest technological advancement. Instead, emphasis is placed on questions of long-term software life expectancy, rather than short-term user satisfaction or temporary software improvements.

A special thank you to my parents for teaching me the joy of learning and the value of education. Also, a sincere thank you to my husband, William, for his encouragement and his editorial advice on the manuscript.

I am indebted to SAMI, a subsidiary company of Time, Inc., Planmetrics Inc., and the Blue Cross Association for many of my software project experiences and for many discussions on software engineering in practice.

Carma L. McClure

Contents

Preface vii

PART 1: INTRODUCTION

1 Software: State of the Art 1
2 Software Development Case Histories: A Failure and a Success 7
   2.1 Introduction 7
   2.2 A Failure 8
   2.3 A Success 13
   2.4 Comparison of the GIRG and the SMCS Projects 22
   2.5 Summary 26

PART 2: MANAGING SOFTWARE DEVELOPMENT

3 Developing Software with Maintenance in Mind 29
   3.1 Introduction 29
   3.2 Software Development Principles 31
   3.3 Software Development Process 37
   3.4 Summary 68
4 Organizing the Software Development Team 70
   4.1 Introduction 70
   4.2 Project Team Organizations 73
   4.3 Revised Chief Programmer Team 81
   4.4 Summary 90
5 Controlling Software Development 92
   5.1 Introduction 92
   5.2 Project Responsibilities 93
   5.3 Project Control Mechanisms 99
   5.4 Change Control 125
   5.5 Summary 130

PART 3: MANAGING SOFTWARE MAINTENANCE

6 Applying Software Engineering to Software Maintenance 133
   6.1 Introduction 133
   6.2 Maintenance 136
   6.3 Performing Maintenance 138
   6.4 Summary 160

7 Controlling Software Maintenance 163
   7.1 Introduction 163
   7.2 Maintenance Teams 164
   7.3 Controlling Software Changes 174
   7.4 Summary 181

PART 4: CONCLUSION

8 Evaluating the Software Life Cycle 185
   8.1 Studying Software Projects 185
   8.2 Evaluating a Software Product 188
   8.3 Evaluating the Software Life Cycle Process 189

Chapter Notes 191

Bibliography 197

Index 199

MANAGING SOFTWARE DEVELOPMENT AND MAINTENANCE

Part 1
Introduction

1
Software: State of the Art

The programming problems we face today are surprisingly similiar to those we faced in the sixties and to those we can anticipate in the eighties.[1] Most software projects fail. Schedules and cost estimates are usually overrun; software seldom meets user expectations or requirements; production systems are never executed error-free.

In the 1960s we began to recognize the difficulty of building and maintaining software, identifying this era as the Software Crisis. Since that time there has been a great deal of effort devoted to the development of software principles and methodologies with most work directed toward the technical aspects of software production. The field of Software Engineering emerged to study software development and maintenance problems.

Perhaps the greatest advancement made so far is a change in attitude toward programming itself. In the 1950s we viewed programming as a simple task whose function was to encode a computation; in the 1960s we viewed it as a difficult, individual skill; and today we see programming as a complex, team-oriented, problem-solving discipline. Structured programming is representative of our change in attitude. Although there is disagreement on whether structured programming is a single concept or an aggregate of methodologies, we do agree that it has helped direct attention toward the need for introducing discipline into programming.

When it was first introduced to industry in the early 1970s structured programming was defined as a set of coding conventions whose function was to standardize the form of the source code. Next structured programming was described as the top-down, step-wise refinement process of designing, coding and testing a hierarchically ordered software system. Today structured programming refers to methodologies that impose a discipline on each stage of the software life cycle and on the organization of the software development team.

The evolution of the definition of structured programming illustrates the beginnings of a broadening concern for management as well as technical problems in software projects, and for the entire software life cycle as well as for the software development phases.

During the past decade, we have learned a great deal about software engineering. Principles and methodologies have been established for developing software systems. In project after project we have found that following these principles has kept us on schedule, has improved the correctness and quality of the software produced and has increased our chances for project success. For example, IBM studies report an average of 40 percent productivity savings in real-time, business, and systems software projects utilizing structured programming.[2]

In other projects, however, we have found that the principles of software engineering do not always guarantee success. Some frequent observations include the following:

- Coding standards cannot improve program quality if they are not enforced by management.
- Top-down design is a general and ambiguous concept that is difficult to apply in practice.
- The chief programmer team concept does not fit many data processing organizations because few qualified chief programmers exist.
- Structured programming cannot ensure project success when it is used as a substitute for good project management.
- Programmer attitude can greatly affect project success.
- Software projects are often out of control because management does not know whether to treat programmers as artisans or engineers.
- Software engineering does not address user needs or software maintenance support.
- Case histories of past software projects are not available for study.

Statistics gathered from industry show that we have a great deal more to learn about software engineering. The cost of software is continuing to rise with the greatest portion of effort and cost spent after software development and during software maintenance. In the past decade programmer productivity has increased by one order of magnitude, but hardware costs have dropped by over two orders of magnitude. Software costs now constitute 70 percent of automation costs.[3] In 1973 U.S. software costs were $20 billion[4] and are projected to be $200 billion in 1985.[5]

Industry surveys show that 70 percent of the total system cost[6] and 40 to 95 percent of the manpower effort in typical industrial applications occurs during software maintenance.[7] A shocking, but hopefully atypical, example from a recent Department of Defense Study reports that development costs for Air Force avionics software average $75 per instruction while maintenance costs lie in the range of $4000 per instruction.[8]

Most software engineering methodologies and tools concentrate on the technical aspects of new software development. On the other hand, relatively few tools have been developed for managing software projects or for maintaining existing systems. Past projects and current cost trends point out that these areas also merit attention. In a 1978 survey of data processing managers from both manufacturing and nonmanufacturing industries, management issues were viewed as more important than technical issues and maintenance of existing systems as more important than new development projects.[9]

Data processing traditionally has been treated as an isolated part of the total company. Because data processing is not well understood by management, it is not subject to the same management controls and scrutiny as other departments. Data processing personnel are treated differently and separately from other personnel. Few data processing managers have had formal management training. They do not show an interest in overall corporate goals, and few attempts are made to integrate them into the overall corporate structure. Data processing management seldom migrate into other areas of a company or rise to nontechnical upper-level management positions. Instead, both data processing managers and personnel migrate from data processing department to data processing department in various companies. According to a recent study, the average turnover time for a programmer is three years.[10] This high rate adversely affects continuity in software development and maintenance efforts. The lack of integration with the total corporate structure makes data processing personnel oblivious to the existence of the user. Software is seen as an abstract structure whose quality lies in its form rather than in its utility. The emphasis of structured programming and software engineering on technical issues is a good example of this attitude.

Traditionally, maintenance has been treated as an activity separate from new development. Usually, maintenance efforts are staffed by different and less experienced data processing personnel than new development projects. Until project turnover, there is little interaction between the two groups. Within data processing circles there is a stigma attached to maintenance, which is viewed as a nonchallenging environment offering little opportunity to gain expertise with current technologies. Software engineering is not thought applicable to the maintenance environment. With a growing number of complex systems to be maintained and with the use of few advanced software tools, maintenance problems and likewise maintenance costs are increasing.

The objective of this book is to apply the principles of software engineering to maintaining existing software systems. When the software life cycle is discussed in courses and at seminars, we often hear the guideline to develop with maintenance in mind. This is sound advice, but what does it really mean? How do the system developer and the system maintainer implement this guideline in practice? We shall answer these questions by:

- Adapting the standards and procedures successfully used in new development to software maintenance support.
- Addressing software maintenance support issues during the software development process.
- Defining communication mechanisms between software developers, maintainers and users.

We conclude this chapter with a list of general guidelines for software development. We divide the list into three categories: technical guidelines, product control guidelines, and project control guidelines. In the chapters that follow we shall discuss these guidelines and adapt them to the maintenance environment. Our emphasis will center on the second and third categories since there already are many books devoted to the technical aspects of software engineering.

In Part II of this book, we shall review the basic principles of software engineering and the software life cycle in preparation for utilizing them in the maintenance environment. Also, we shall refine the software life cycle to include preparations for software support. We shall not treat software development and maintenance as completely separate activities since they will share principles and techniques and exchange personnel.

In Part III, we shall concentrate on software maintenance with particular attention to the management aspects of software maintenance. We shall look at how the maintenance manager prepares to perform the maintenance function, organizes the maintenance staff, and interacts with the user.

We shall conclude in Part IV with a discussion of the final phase of the software life cycle, and an evaluation of the project and the product success based upon the goals established at project inception.

GUIDELINES FOR SOFTWARE DEVELOPMENT[11]

1. Technical Guidelines

    1.1 Use automated tools such as well-engineered operating systems, preprocessors, packages, cross reference generators, documentation generators, test generators, source management systems, etc.
    1.2 Use structured programming.
    1.3 Use a combination top-down/bottom-up design approach.
    1.4 Develop a test plan at design time.
    1.5 Use higher order languages.
    1.6 Strive for machine independence and code compatibility with language standards.
    1.7 Opt for "people" efficiency over machine efficiency.
    1.8 Keep a repository of common modules.
    1.9 Survey successful software engineering techniques and adopt them.

2. Product Control Guidelines

   2.1 At project initiation divide the system into pieces defining requirements, a test plan, and milestones.
   2.2 Design for off-nominal inputs.
   2.3 Design with maintenance in mind.
   2.4 Strive for simplicity rather than completeness.
   2.5 Periodically review the project, performing explicit validation procedures and audit controls.
   2.6 Involve the user in reviews.
   2.7 Produce user documentation early in the project.

3. Project Control Guidelines

   3.1 Develop a project plan and use it to manage the project.
   3.2 Explicitly define project goals and priorities.
   3.3 Produce clear, concise statements of user requirements to be reviewed periodically in greater and greater detail with the user.
   3.4 Use fewer and better people to staff the development team.
   3.5 Maintain clear accountability of each individual team member for results enabling him to gage his performance.
   3.6 Set up career paths, salary scales and benefits to reward high performers.
   3.7 Do not use structured programming as a substitute for good management.
   3.8 Develop program libraries for project management.
   3.9 Evaluate project success in terms of its goals.

2
Software Development Case Histories: A Failure and a Success

2.1 INTRODUCTION

Why do some software projects succeed and others fail? We in industry experience many software failures and are discovering that management problems often outweigh technical problems.

There are three basic ingredients necessary for project success:

1. technical tools
2. technical expertise
3. management techniques

Ignoring any one of these ingredients will greatly increase the risk of project failure. We have focused most of our attention on the first two ingredients. Great advancements have been made in the technical areas with the introduction of structured programming, design techniques, automated test tools, etc. On the other hand, we have paid relatively little attention to good project management, especially in very large projects because they have been a management impossibility and in small projects because they did not merit the project management overhead.

In this chapter, we illustrate the dangers of underestimating the need for project management by presenting the case histories of two software development projects from industry. In the first project, the available technical tools and the management techniques proved inadequate; in the second, following the principles of software engineering led to project success. When we compare the two projects, we shall observe that, although both project teams advocated software

8   PART 1   INTRODUCTION

engineering, they differed in their management approach. This ultimately made the difference between project success and failure.

First, we shall discuss the two projects, examining the probable reasons for failure and for success. Then, we shall compare the projects using the General Guidelines for Software Development presented in Chapter 1. Finally, we shall conclude by re-emphasizing the value of employing sound software engineering practices in all software projects regardless of their size or their familiarity.

2.2   A FAILURE

2.2.1   History of the IFMS-I Report Generator Project*

IFMS-I is an interactive system used in building financial planning models. It provides a nontechnical user with a set of interactive commands allowing easy input of data, manipulation of variables over time periods, and production of reports. IFMS-I resides on an XDS-940 computer. It was developed in the early 1970s and was primarily written in an XDS dialect of FORTRAN II.

The objective of the IFMS-I Report Generator Project (GIRG) was to develop a major enhancement to IFMS-I by adding a Report Generator Subsystem. The new report generator would expand the report editing and formatting capabilities currently available to the IFMS-I user. The project was instigated by management to continue interest in an eight-year-old software product whose second-generation limitations were becoming more and more apparent with the advent of hardware/software advances. The top priority concerns of management were:

1. to develop the enhancement as soon as possible
2. to make the enhancement compatible with the current IFMS-I system and existing models so no or very little user retraining would be necessary

During an initial study, the Systems and Programming Group estimated that the GIRG Project would be an eight-man-month effort.

---

*Although the projects and the software products are real, the names used in this chapter are fictitious.

The estimate was based upon a recently completed project (IFMS–III) in which the IFMS–I system was converted (with major enhancements) to reside on a PRIME 300 minicomputer. Since the IFMS–I Report Generator was to be patterned after the IFMS–III Report Generator, the system requirements were clearly defined.

The study warned that the GIRG project could be adversely affected by developing software on the outdated XDS-940 computer. System documentation for IFMS–I was scarce, and XDS-940 operating system documentation was even more scarce. The Systems and Programming Group had no individual with previous XDS-940 development experience. To alleviate this problem, management hired a member of the original IFMS–I development team as a consultant to teach IFMS–I and XDS–940 system internals to the GIRG project team.

The GIRG project began in February 1978 and was scheduled for completion in July 1978. The project team consisted of three members: a project leader, a programmer, and the consultant. The project leader was the former project leader from the successful IFMS-III project. He was familiar with the IFMS modeling system concept and the user requirements, but had little experience with the XDS-940 system internals which are peculiar to the 940. The programmer was a new employee knowledgeable in FORTRAN IV but unfamiliar with IFMS–I and the XDS-940.

Although the consultant was hired to teach 940 internals to the project team, he preferred to design the Report Generator Subsystem. The project leader who had no formal management training felt that his authority was challenged and, perhaps for this reason, assumed a less active management role in the project. The programmer developed a split loyalty between his teacher and his project leader. The result was three design definitions: the design defined by the consultant, the design redefined by the project leader to be more compatible with management objectives, and finally, the design as interpreted by the programmer.

The design disputes coupled with the fact that the project tasks were not defined in detail made the project difficult to control. Weekly status meetings were held, but open communication was stifled. System components became the sole property of an individual rather than the team. When problems occurred, the team members could not help one another because they would not cross "territorial boundaries."

2.2.2 Evaluation of the GIRG Project

The GIRG project failed. The Report Generator Subsystem was not completed until December 1978, causing the cancellation of new product demonstrations and the rescheduling of pilot modeling projects.

Why did the project fail? The factors contributing to the delinquency of the project lie in both the technical and the management areas.

In the technical area, problems arose due to inadequate software development tools. Specifically, these problems included:

- a second-generation, unfamiliar computer system
- poor-to-nonexistent system documentation
- nonstandard programming language
- poor debugging facility and text editor

The initial study had pointed out these problem areas, but their ramifications had been underestimated and proper scheduling adjustments had not been made. Hiring a consultant to supplement inadequate documentation was not enough to compensate for antiquated technical tools. Providing third-generation programmers with only second-generation tools, without allowing for a significant adjustment/training period, greatly contributed to project failure. First, the programmers required information on the XDS-940 operating system since the IFMS software interfaced with the operating system to capture interrupts and to handle terminal I/O functions. Also, the development of several NARP (XDS-940 Assembly Language) routines was necessary. Since neither detailed written documentation nor adequate verbal assistance was available from the vendor or the consultant, the program development effort was reduced to a "let's try it and see what happens" approach. This, of course, costs time. Second, the XDS FORTRAN was not only nonstandard but also substandard since it did not include the control structures normally found in standard FORTRAN. For example, there was no logical If statement.

SOFTWARE DEVELOPMENT CASE HISTORIES: A FAILURE AND A SUCCESS 11

This too costs time. Third, the debugging tools hindered rather than helped development. The trace facility introduced errors into the program causing further schedule problems and frustrations.

In the project management area, poor management judgment and compromises contributed to the project failure. In general, project management was lax, ignoring the basic principles of software engineering.[1] Because the project was small and the application was well-understood, it was rationalized that only an informal management structure was needed. There was no formal project plan, no schedule, no team organization, no clear definition of individual responsibilities. Nothing was written down. All communications, including development philosophy, task assignments, and status reports, were verbal. Violations of the principles of software engineering included:

- incomplete specifications
- no top-down design approach
- no definition of project tasks
- no definition of project milestones
- no scheduled training

System-level specifications and user documentation were produced at the outset of the project. However, detailed specifications were never written; instead detailed programming immediately began. A top-down design approach was not followed; instead a bottom-up, piece-by-piece approach with no interface planning was used. Project tasks were not defined in terms of man-effort or formally assigned. Milestones for measuring progress were not laid out. Finally, training time for the new programmer was not included in the schedule.

Although both technical and management problems were experienced, the management problems were by far the more serious. The lack of formal structure made it impossible to control the GIRG project, to estimate the impact of problems, and to handle the personality conflicts that arose.

If the GIRG project were repeated, it would be managed very differently. The following suggestions could produce improved results:

1. Establish the project leader's authority at the beginning of the project by making him directly responsible for a written

project plan, detail specifications and status reporting, and by reinforcing his decision-making authority throughout the project.
2. Train the programmer as an IFMS-I system user before teaching him any XDS-940 internals. Understanding how a system is to be used is a necessary prerequisite to building it.
3. Engage the consultant to teach XDS-940 internals after the programmer has become an experienced IFMS-I user and after the overview specifications for the Report Generator Subsystem were defined. Since the project leader would have had the opportunity to design the system and convey his philosophy to the programmer, he should not feel that his authority is challenged by the outsider entering the project at this point. Also, he would be in a better position to control the consultant.
4. Lay out a detailed project task schedule containing man-effort estimates and assignments that could be used to track the project on a weekly basis.
5. Lay out a detailed test plan during the design phase.
6. Do not allow one project team member to be solely knowledgeable of any part of the system.
7. Use a combination top-down/bottom-up approach so testing could begin early in the project.

2.2.3 Conclusions from the GIRG Project

Now that we have analyzed the GIRG project, have cited probable reasons for its failure, and have listed ways in which the project could have been better managed, we must still ask a few more questions to understand why this project failed and why its failure could not be prevented.

First, since the team understood the principles of software engineering and had successfully applied them in previous projects, why did the team choose not to use them in this project? I have already stated that they believed that it was not necessary because this was a small project, because they were in a hurry and because they knew they could build a report generator. After all, they had done that and much more in the IFMS-III project. There is a more subtle, yet more important reason: the Systems and Programming Group did not want to do the GIRG project. It did not present a challenge since it was a subset of a problem that they had recently solved. It was an enhancement to a second-generation system which in their opinion should be replaced by the IFMS-III system. It would not further develop their technical expertise since they would not be working with state-of-the-art tools.

This observation suggests other questions we should ask. Should we consider a project team a group of professionals or craftsmen? If we view them as professionals, is it necessary for them to agree with a project to be expected to work on it? If we view them as craftsmen, how much can attitudes and personalities affect project success? Is selling a project to the development team, so it will be viewed as exciting, challenging, and worthwhile, a part of the managment function?

In the GIRG project, management did not believe that it was necessary to explain how the project fit into the overall corporate goals. The Systems and Programming Group viewed itself as an isolated group whose career paths did not cross into other parts of the organization and whose major interest was in software engineering, not corporate goals. These attitudes contributed to the lack of team spirit and interest in the project and were the most important factors that doomed the project to failure.

2.3 A SUCCESS

2.3.1 History of the SMCS Charting Project

The purpose of the SMCS Charting Project was to produce a graphics system to report sales trends in grocery products.

The system resided on an IBM 370 computer interfacing with a Beta Cóm Plotter to produce the graphics output. It was written in ANS COBOL with minimal use of IBM assembly language. The project schedule included three months to produce the first chart format and eight months to complete the entire system. The SMCS project begin in June 1974 and was scheduled for completion in February 1975.

The SMCS project team consisted of five members—four programmers and one user liaison. Technical expertise among the programmers

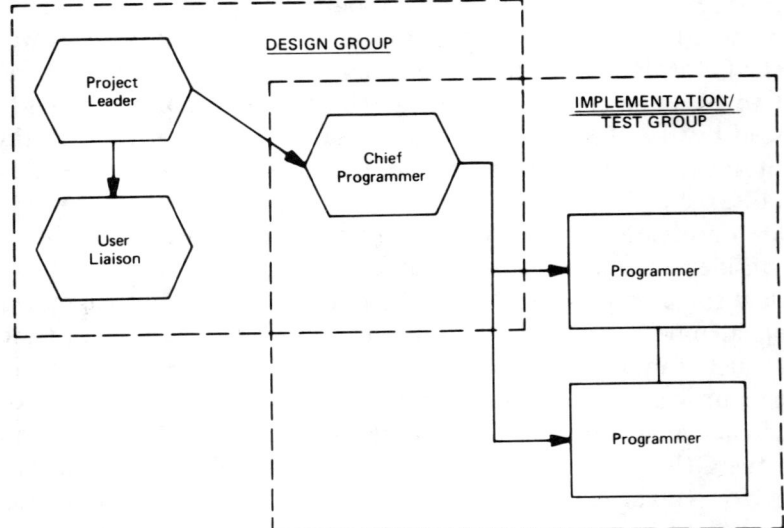

Fig. 2.1. SMCS project team organization.

ranged from six months to six years of business applications programming experience. None of the team members previously had worked together.

Team member responsibilities were patterned after the Chief Programmer Team Concept.[2] One member functioned as the project manager whose duties included managerial responsibilities and program design. The liaison member clarified project specification requirements for both the team and the user. A third member acted as the chief programmer and the remaining two members served as the implementation programmers. The chief programmer participated in the system design and directed the implementation and testing efforts. The implementation programmers were responsible for coding and testing the program.

The SMCS project team was divided into two work groups:

1. Design Group
2. Implementation/Test Group

SOFTWARE DEVELOPMENT CASE HISTORIES: A FAILURE AND A SUCCESS

The Design Group included the project manager, the user liaison and the chief programmer. The Implementation/Test Group was composed of the chief programmer and the two implementation programmers (see Fig. 2.1).

At the outset of the project, the team defined its project goals as follows:
- to develop reliable programs within the time schedule proposed by management
- to develop programs that met user requirements and were easily modifiable
- to write well-structured programs

The software techniques that the team selected to develop the SMCS system were:
- a top-down design approach
- implementation in structured COBOL[3]
- a top-down testing approach

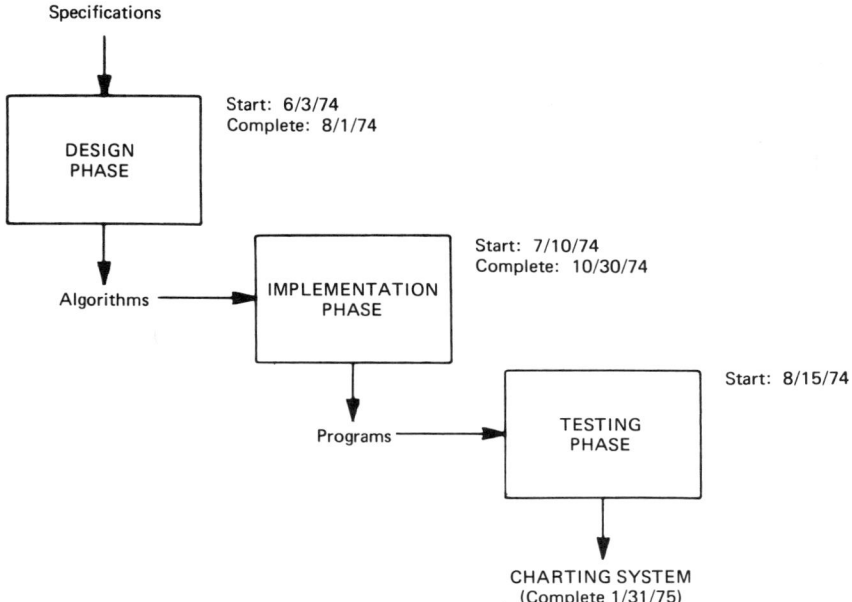

Fig. 2.2. SMCS project schedule.

The team also decided to evaluate the utility of these techniques as a by-product of the project.

The development process for the SMCS Charting System was divided into the traditional phases of design, implementation, and testing. The phases were not treated as strict sequential steps in that they were allowed to overlap (see Fig. 2.2).

Although the design process began in a top-down fashion, the SMCS Charting System design was not developed in a strict top-down manner. This was the result of selecting the hardest-first strategy to order design decisions (i.e., address the most conceptually difficult design decisions first).[4] For example, because chart scaling was considered the most conceptually difficult part of the system, it was designed first and the design for the rest of the system components grew out from it (see Fig. 2.3).

The output of the design phase was a set of hierarchical program segments able to perform the system requirements. The definition of a program segment was expressed as an algorithm composed of two parts:

1. necessary information
2. processing procedure

The necessary information listed the variables accessed in a program segment. Each program variable was associated with either a table or a work-area. If it were part of a table, the variable could be accessed anywhere in the program; if it were part of the work-area, it was accessed exclusively by the program segment. The processing procedure outlined in sequential steps a process performing the segment task. The formation of a program module was directed by these processing steps. Each step represented a module or hierarchy of program modules depending upon the complexity of the implementation.

The design of an algorithm proceeded in the following manner. First, the Design Group abstracted away exceptions to reveal common processing characteristics for any chart and from this built an algorithm for the general case. Next, the Design Group expanded the general case to include special processing considerations peculiar to a particular chart format. The Design Group believed that consistently adhering to this design approach would preserve system integrity.

SOFTWARE DEVELOPMENT CASE HISTORIES: A FAILURE AND A SUCCESS   17

Design decisions were influenced by considerations of how each program segment interfaced with the rest of the program. The objective was to make each interface simple and obvious to reduce complexity. To the Design Group this meant having each segment access as few control variables as possible. No segment was defined without

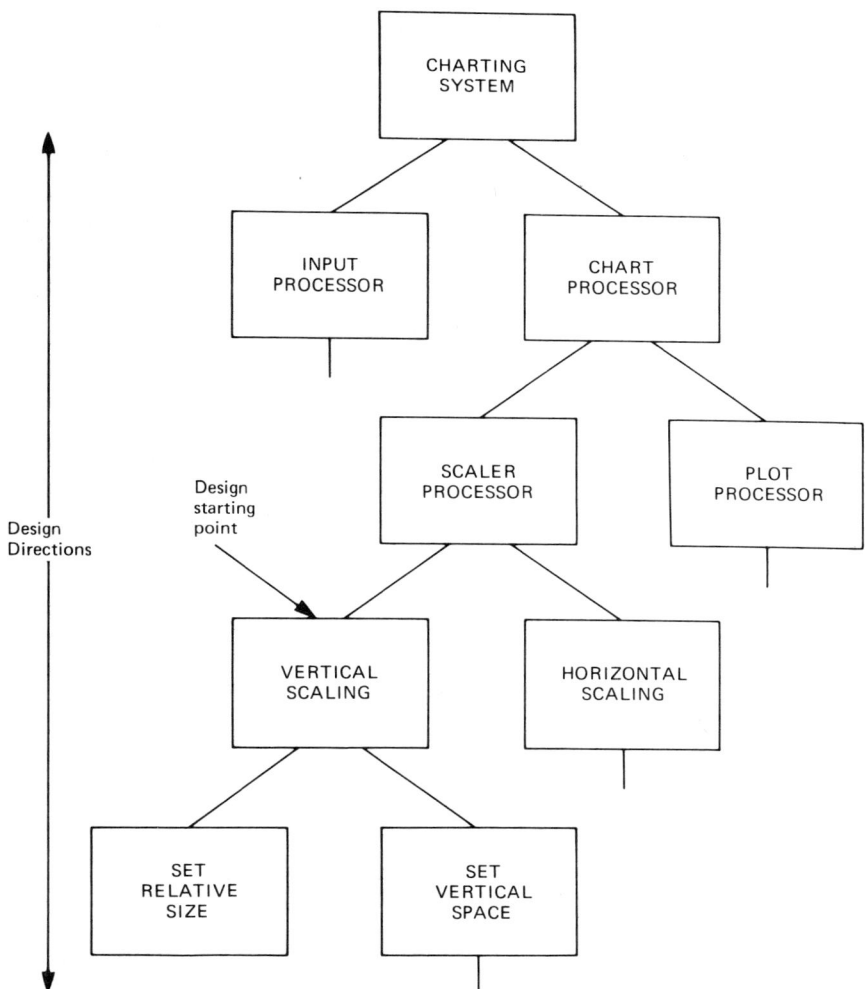

Fig. 2.3. Combination top-down/bottom-up design for SMCS Project

examining its relationship to the overall program structure. It was designed as an independent procedural component whose internal processing could be modified with minimal effect on the rest of the program.

The SMCS Charting System was not coded in a strict top-down manner since the implementation order was established by the design order of working with the hardest parts first. The Implementation/Test Group was responsible for transforming the design into a well-structured program meeting specification requirements. The chief programmer assigned coding tasks consisting of the implementation of a program segment design. The design algorithm for the program segment served as the major source of program specification material for the programmer. The programmer's task was to implement the algorithm as a hierarchy of structured COBOL modules, to coordinate implementation efforts with other programmers, and to report any design errors discovered during the implementation. Although the procedural steps in the algorithm offered a possible modularization scheme, final modularization decisions for the implementation were left to the discretion of the programmer.

Implementation was not considered an individual effort; instead, the Implementation/Test Group viewed it as a team effort. The chief programmer wrote no code, but reviewed all code, checking to see that it met specification requirements and that it complied with structured coding conventions. The programmers were encouraged to discuss implementation techniques and problems they encountered in using structured COBOL.

The Testing Phase of the SMCS project included two types of traditional testing:

1. Unit Testing
2. System Testing

Unit testing was performed for each program segment to show that the segment correctly executed its task. When all unit testing was satisfactorily completed, system testing began. There was no integration testing phase as such. The objective of system testing was to show that the entire system functioned properly.

SOFTWARE DEVELOPMENT CASE HISTORIES: A FAILURE AND A SUCCESS   19

The chief programmer directed the Testing Phase. The implementation programmers served as the actual testers. To ensure testing objectivity, the programmer who coded a segment usually was not assigned the task of testing that segment. Before beginning unit testing for a particular segment, the tester was required to present a test plan to the chief programmer. It included:

- the testing approach (e.g., selection of live or dummy data)
- a list of test cases
- anticipated results for each test case

No actual strategy was used in selecting test cases. The Testing Group simply used the intuitive approach of covering as many program paths as possible. After the test plan was approved, the tester performed unit testing until all test cases had been correctly executed according to anticipated results. The chief programmer then reviewed the results to determine that unit testing was successfully completed.

Although system testing was primarily the responsibility of the chief programmer, every member of the project team participated. The Design Group selected the test cases and obtained the input data for system tests; the Test Group executed the tests; the chief programmer directed result checking and determined when the program was functionally correct.

2.3.2 Evaluation of the SMCS Project

The SMCS Project began in June 1974 and was completed on schedule in February 1975. The system contained 17,279 lines of code, including four COBOL subroutines and five assembly language routines. Only 90 lines of code were written in assembly language.

The programmer productivity rate for the project was 21.6 debugged lines per program or per day. This rate was calculated using a time span of eight months for four programmers. The user liaison did no coding.

Since February 1975, the SMCS Charting System has been used as a production program that runs on a four-week cycle. During its first two years in production, only two errors occurred.

The SMCS project was considered successful for several reasons:

1. It was completed on schedule.
2. The programmers achieved a very satisfactory productivity rate.
3. The SMCS system is a reliable production system.
4. The SMCS system is well-structured.
5. The SMCS project team achieved its goals.

The project succeeded primarily because it used a systematic, disciplined approach to software development. Individual responsibilities and detailed project tasks were carefully defined, making project control and tracking possible. Potential problems were recognized early and corrected before they adversely affected the project schedule.

A secondary factor leading to success was the team's evaluation of the software engineering techniques used in the project. It is interesting to note that several observations made by the team point out deficiencies in software tools that still exist today.

First, their design observations showed that a strict top-down design approach was not suitable for all design problems. Had they not used a combination top-down/bottom-up approach, the Design Group believed that they could not have completed the system on schedule. Also, the design objective was to produce a well-structured system in which complexity was minimized. The properties of a well-structured program were clear, but the notion of program complexity was vague. The Design Group found no design technique to measure and reduce program complexity.

Second, the SMCS project team's reaction to using structured COBOL coding conventions was very positive. The programmers observed that the coding conventions forced a standardization of style that made the program easier to understand. This standardization increased their confidence in working with parts of the system that had been designed or coded by other team members.

Third, the team found existing software testing tools inadequate. There were tools available to generate and to check test data, but no techniques to help structure the testing process. Since it is not possible to test all cases, the team's testing objective was to concentrate the testing effort on the normal processing cases and on the most complex parts of the program. A test strategy specifically tailored to pinpoint program complexity was needed, but no such techniques were known.

2.3.3 Conclusions from the SMCS Project

Allowing the team members to participate in the selection and evaluation of software development techniques helped to create a team spirit and an excitement for the project. Each member believed that the project presented him with an opportunity to broaden his expertise, to contribute to the development of company standards and procedures, and to be recognized by management. This tended to raise egos from an individual level to a team level. Criticisms were directed toward software engineering techniques rather than toward individuals. There were no secrets in the project; the design specifications, the code, and the tests belonged to everyone. This resulted in the team's ability to uncover errors early in the project and to remain on schedule.

It is difficult to estimate the impact that cultivating a team spirit had on the project. I believe that it was great. A second SMCS project supports this belief.

2.3.4 SMCS Revision Project

During the summer of 1975, revisions were made to the SMCS Charting System in preparation for an expanded charting application. The revision team consisted of the chief programmer from the first SMCS project and two junior programmers (hereafter referred to as Programmer I and Programmer II). Programmer I and Programmer II each had less than one year of programming experience and had not been members of the first SMCS project team.

The revision team was organized in the same manner as the first SMCS project team. The chief programmer wrote the modification specifications and directed all coding and testing efforts of the junior programmers.

The revisions were divided into two groups each of which contained several programming tasks. It was necessary to complete Group I tasks before beginning Group II tasks. The chief programmer assigned Programmer II the more difficult tasks in Group I and then assigned Pro-

22 PART 1 INTRODUCTION

Table 2.1. Programmer Productivity for SMCS Revision Project

REVISIONS	PROGRAMMER	TIME SPENT	LINES CODED	PRODUCTIVITY
Group I	I	6 weeks	375	12.5
	II	5 weeks	983	39.3
Group II	I	5 weeks	1302	52.1
	II	5 weeks	126	5.0

grammer I the more difficult tasks in Group II. In this way, he could distribute time between the two programmers and concentrate on the more difficult revisions. Also, this created a good learning environment for each programmer.

The charting revisions consisted of 2786 lines of code that were written and tested over a three month period. They were completed on schedule. The programmer productivity rates are shown in Table 2.1. The overall programmer productivity rate for the project was 25.3 lines per programmer per day. If support programs (3396) that were coded to test Group II revisions are also included, the productivity rate is increased to 56.2.

An interesting observation comes to view when each programmer's productivity is considered separately. The productivity for each programmer varied greatly between Group I and Group II revisions. This was an unexpected result. For both programmers, the higher productivity rate was for the more difficult tasks. According to the programmers, they did not find the easier programming tasks interesting and they preferred to work with close supervision from the chief programmer on challenging tasks. Again, we see that individual attitude and preference can greatly affect a project.

2.4 COMPARISON OF THE GIRG AND THE SMCS PROJECTS

Now that we have reviewed the GIRG and SMCS project histories, we shall compare them using the Guidelines for Software Development presented in Chapter 1. Intuitively, we expect that the SMCS project followed the guidelines to a much greater degree than did the GIRG project. To test our intuition, we assign a software engineering score to each project. For each guideline followed, we add one to the project score; for each guideline partially followed we add one-half to the score. Table 2.2 shows the software engineering score for each project. The maximum possible score is 25.

The software engineering score for the GIRG project is 7, while the software engineering score for the SMCS project is 16.5. Examining the scores more closely, we see that the GIRG project disregarded fourteen of the twenty-five guidelines, and of the eleven followed, eight were only partially followed. The SMCS project employed nineteen guidelines. Of these nineteen, five were partially followed. The lowest score for the GIRG project was in the technical category; the lowest score for the SMCS project was in the project control category.

In the technical category, the GIRG project complied with only one guideline. FORTRAN rather than XDS 940 assembly language was used whenever possible because FORTRAN is easier to maintain than the poorly documented 940 assembly language. None of the other technical guidelines were followed in the GIRG project because the 940 system did not provide adequate technical tools and because the project team believed that the project was too small to benefit from structured programming techniques.

On the other hand, the SMCS project complied with all but one technical guideline. Since the SMCS application was unique among other applications, a repository of common modules was not kept. Two technical guidelines were only partially followed in the SMCS project. First, although automated software development tools such as a source management system and test data generators were used, other tools such as structure checking preprocessors were not readily available five years ago. Second, since the team did not understand how to structure the testing process, only an ad hoc test plan was developed.

The product control score for the SMCS project was higher than for the GIRG project. In the SMCS project, five out of seven guidelines were followed. One of the five was only partially followed because the team did not know how to design with maintenance in mind. They believed that striving for understandability of the code and consistency in the design would simplify future maintenance efforts. As an example of this philosophy, the system was designed so that all charts formats were plotted from left to right and from top to bottom,

Table 2.2. Software Engineering Scores for GIRG and SMCS Projects

	GIRG PROJECT	SMCS PROJECT
TECHNICAL GUIDELINES		
1.1		.5
1.2		1.0
1.3		1.0
1.4		.5
1.5	1.0	1.0
1.6	.5	1.0
1.7		1.0
1.8		
1.9		1.0
Total	1.5	7
Product Control Guidelines		
2.1	.5	1.0
2.2	1.0	1.0
2.3	.5	.5
2.4		1.0
2.5		1.0
2.6	.5	.5
2.7	.5	
Total	3	5
Project Control Guidelines		
3.1		
3.2	.5	1.0
3.3	.5	.5
3.4	.5	
3.5		1.0
3.6		
3.7		1.0
3.8		
3.9		1.0
Total	2.5	4.5
Software Engineering Score	7	16.5

regardless of machine efficiency loss for some formats. Also, the team believed that simplicity should outweigh completeness as a design goal since they could not anticipate all future requirements. The team did not follow the guideline to include the user in reviews or to produce user documentation early in the project. Management did not allow any direct user contact with the team. This was a mistake because the team had little understanding of how the system would actually be used.

In the GIRG project, most product control guidelines were followed to some degree. Although no milestones or test plan were defined, the user requirements were carefully defined and reviewed with the user at the beginning of the project. The requirements were written in the form of a first draft of the user documentation. The team's top priority goal was to design and to implement the new subsystem so it would not affect the currently operational system pieces. However, without product standards, it was not possible to use audit controls and reviews.

The project control score for the SMCS project also was higher than for the GIRG project. Six out of ten project control guidelines were followed in the SMCS project. No formal project plan was developed but project goals, quality control standards, and a task schedule were established. The project team was given no choice in the assignment of personnel, but individual responsibilities and assignments were carefully decided upon among team members. An automated project management system was not used since the project was small.

Only half of the project control guidelines were followed in the GIRG project. No project plan was developed. Although management priorities were clear, they were not adopted as the GIRG team goals. The user was consulted only during an initial requirement definition phase. Since the task assignments were verbal, it was difficult to evaluate each individual's performance.

Using the software engineering score as an indicator of the probability of project failure, we expect the risk of project failure to be much higher in the GIRG project than in the SMCS project. This, of course, proved to be true. We are not, however, suggesting that the software engineering score can be used as a complete predictor of the probability of project failure. We are suggesting that a project manager examine a project's adherence to the general software guidelines.

Each guideline that is not followed should be investigated and justified in terms of project priorities, available tools and cost considerations. Since these are only general guidelines, every rule will not fit every project. However, managers should be especially suspect of projects with a very low software engineering score. As we saw in the GIRG project, it is very easy to rationalize that there is no need for formality or software engineering in small projects or familiar applications. We found that this reasoning is indeed dangerous and can lead to project failure. Also, we suggest that project managers build a data base of project software engineering scores. Studying past projects will establish the validity of the guidelines and will identify which guidelines are particularly important in their environment.

2.5 SUMMARY

In this chapter, we examined two software development projects. The major differences between the two lie in the utility of software engineering techniques and project management. The results, as measured by the project software engineering score, point out that ignoring the guidelines for software development can increase the risk of project failure. They also point out that the attitude of a project team toward a project can affect its outcome. Besides understanding the technical principles of software development, we must understand and plan for the human aspects. As project managers, we must learn to "sell" a project to the project development team as well as to the user. It is an even more serious management problem in software maintenance efforts than in new development projects because of the stigma attached to the maintenance function. In Part III, we shall turn our attention to this problem.

Part 2
Managing Software Development

3
Developing Software with Maintenance in Mind

3.1 INTRODUCTION

In Part II, we study software development. However, our purpose is different than in most other software engineering texts. We do not view software development as an end in itself; instead, we look at the entire software life cycle with our attention focused on the last phase —operation and maintenance. We explore in depth the question of how to develop software with maintenance in mind.

Our reason for viewing software development in terms of maintainability is based upon current state of the art problems. As we pointed out in Part I, software costs greatly exceed hardware costs.

> Software costs as a percentage of total system costs have systematically risen from less than 20 percent to more than 80 percent today, and are still growing.[1]

In addition, more time is spent maintaining existing systems than developing new systems.

> ... some 75 percent of data processing personnel are already taken up with maintenance, not development. And unless radical new methods are found, maintenance will go even higher in its demands and will very nearly stifle further development.[2]

In the past, we have assumed that if we improve the software development process and if we learn to produce error-free code, we can control the rising cost of maintenance. Indeed this would be a convenient solution, but is a poor assumption for two reasons. First, there are billions of lines of production code in industry today. This solution does not help us address the problem of maintaining existing software systems. Realistically, we cannot afford to discard these systems, replacing them with well-structured, error-free code, at least in the short term. Second, according to a recent survey, most maintenance effort (82 percent) is spent modifying software to accommodate changes and to improve software performance rather than to correct errors not discovered during system development (18 percent).[3] A solution that focuses upon the production phases of the software life cycle does not address the major portion of the maintenance effort. We have underestimated the impact of change on the software life cycle. We must find a solution to maintenance problems that includes ways in which we can better understand the user, and better prepare for inevitable and continual software change.

We must directly address maintenance issues rather than hope that they will disappear by improving the development process. If we hope to control rising software costs, we can no longer allow a pronounced split in our technology and in our project management between software development and maintenance. The principles of software engineering that we have used to improve the software development project and the software product quality must be adopted for use in the maintenance area. Also, we must refine the software development process to properly prepare for more comprehensive and economical software maintenance.

Part II consists of three chapters. In Chapter 3, we review the software life cycle. As we look at each life cycle phase, we outline steps to take in developing a more maintainable system. For example, we discuss what complexity controls should be applied and what testing statistics should be recorded for the software maintainer as part of a system support profile.

In Chapter 4, we discuss how to organize software development project teams. This is important to us for two reasons. First, we look at how to involve the system maintainer and the user in the development process to ensure the production of a useful, maintainable system. Second, we study the organization of development teams so we can adapt these structures to the organization of a maintenance staff.

In Chapter 5, we discuss controlling software development. This is crucial to us because the control mechanisms used in development phases set the standards for controlling the system throughout its entire life cycle. Of particular importance to us is the discussion of the change control mechanism to be used during development and then adapted for maintenance.

3.2 SOFTWARE DEVELOPMENT PRINCIPLES

3.2.1 Introduction

In this chapter, we concentrate on refining the software development process to ensure maintainability. Because this presupposes that we understand the terms software, software life cycle, and the characteristics of software quality, we begin by reviewing their definitions.

3.2.2 Software

We define *software* as a product consisting of three necessary components:

1. computer program code
2. data
3. documentation[4]

The computer code consists of both source code and executable code. Since data processing applications by definition operate on data, we consider data an essential component of software. Documentation refers to the software system life cycle plan, the program specifications, and the source code documentation.

A software product may be comprised of one or more separate programs. We use the terms software, software system, and system interchangeably.

3.2.3 Software Life Cycle

We define the *software life cycle* as a multiphase process beginning with problem definition and continuing to software system obsolescence. Although we can refine the phases further, the life cycle is typically defined as consisting of six basic phases:

1. Requirements Analysis
2. Specification
3. Design
4. Coding
5. Testing
6. Operation and Maintenance [5]

Requirements analysis is a process whose objective is to define the requirements for a solution to a problem. In some instances, the best solution may not be a computer solution. During requirements analysis the computer is viewed as a possible tool to be used in solving the problem. Resources such as manpower, hardware, and operation personnel needed to create and support the software are considered.

Specification is the process by which each function to be performed by the software is precisely defined. For example, the inputs and outputs to the system and their data structures are defined.

Design is the process by which algorithms are developed to describe how each specified software system function is to be performed. During the design phase, the functional specifications describing what the system is to do, and the system constraints describing the resources available for system use, are studied to produce the design definition.

Coding is the process by which the design algorithms are transformed into computer code. The objective of the coding phase is to perform a translation of the design into code so that the resulting software neither adds to nor subtracts from the design definition.

Testing is the process of demonstrating that the software conforms to specifications and performs correctly for all input data. The goal of testing is to eliminate unexpected program conditions and failures and to discover any incorrect implementation of the specifications.

Operation and Maintenance is the process of executing software in a production mode and keeping software operational. This involves providing operation personnel and computing facilities; correcting errors that were not discovered during testing; and modifying the system to meet changing user needs, to adapt to changes in the operating environment, and to improve operating efficiency.

The life cycle phases are performed sequentially in the order shown in Fig. 3.1. In practice, because of errors and oversights, the phases are often repeated. For example, during the design phase, a specification oversight may be discovered. When this happens, the specification documents must be corrected before the design can continue. Also, in large systems, various phases may be performed in parallel

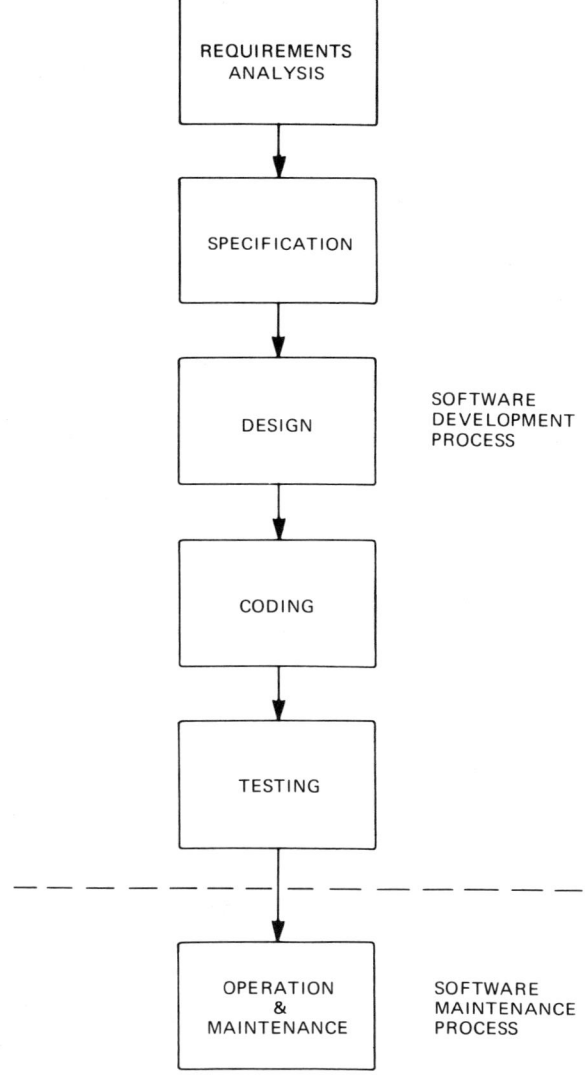

Fig. 3.1. Software life cycle phases.

due to time and cost constraints. For example, the coding and testing of a portion of the system that has already been designed may be in progress while another portion of the system is being designed.

The software development process comprises the first five phases of the life cycle. Since most software engineering research has been directed at these five phases, many principles, methodologies, and tools have been developed to structure this process. Most of the research has been done in the design, coding, and testing phases. Methodologies such as top-down design, structured programming, and structured testing have greatly improved the technical aspects of software production. We will not discuss these methodologies in detail here because there are many good texts available in the subject. We do, however, strongly advocate their use in software development. This was the point of Chapter 2. In this chapter, we shall build upon these methodologies and expand the life cycle development phases to include steps for "building maintainability into" a software system. But before we examine each life cycle phase more closely, we must examine the qualities that a software product should possess and, in particular, we must study the quality of maintainability.

3.2.4 Software Quality Characteristics

The objective of the software development process is to produce a quality product that meets user requirements, that is produced on schedule within cost estimates, and that is easy to operate and to maintain. The issue of software quality has been a difficult question for both the software manager and the software user. How do we measure software quality, and why is it important? In industry, software is meant to be used. In this sense, it is very much like an engineering product rather than a mathematical abstraction. If a software product is not useful to its ultimate user, it is a failure, regardless of its structure, its correctness, or its efficiency.

Although the qualities that a software product should possess vary with the user and the priorities of the user, it is extremely important that these qualities be carefully and explicitly defined early in the software development process. Criteria for measuring software quality should be established and used as guidelines in evaluating software as it is being developed.

Experiments have shown that identifying the software qualities sought and setting priorities for the software developer affect the quality of the software produced. In an experiment conducted by Boehm,[6] two programming efforts were studied. In one effort, the programmer's top priority goal was to maximize the code efficiency. In the second effort, the top priority goal was to emphasize simplicity. The result of this experiment was that ten times as many errors were found in the program produced by the first effort as in the program produced by the second effort. In a programming experiment conducted by Weinberg,[7] the same programming assignment with different top priority goals—such as efficiency, clarity or reduction of the number of source statements—was assigned to different programming groups. The result of this experiment was that each group achieved its highest priority goal.

In the Gen Presentation Project, which followed the completion of the SMCS Charting System, discussed in Chapter 2, Section 2.3, a top priority goal given to the project team was to control program complexity by reducing the number of compares in the code. Essentially the same team worked on this project as on the SMCS Charting Project. The team attempted to accomplish this goal with the following design considerations:

1. Use of control variables, and variables in general, was localized.
2. Logic decisions were not repeated in the same or different modules, when possible.

In comparing the Gen Presentation System with the SMCS Charting System, we found that the average frequency of compares in the source code (source-lines-excluding-comments/number-of-compares) was cut in half in the Gen System. Also, the average number of compares per module was reduced in the Gen Presentation System as compared to the Charting System.[8]

These experiences point out that in the case of software, you can get what you ask for. According to Boehm,[9]

> ... the degree of quality a person puts into a program correlates strongly with the software quality objectives and priorities he has been given.

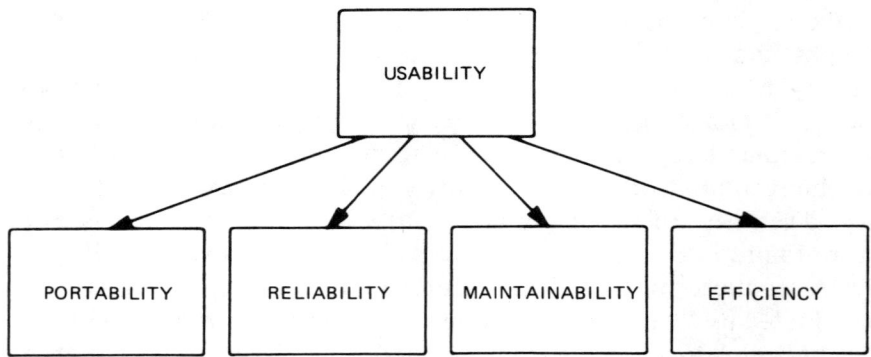

Fig. 3.2. Software quality characteristic hierarchy.

Figure 3.2 shows a subset of the software quality hierarchy as defined by Boehm.[10] Usability is placed at the root of the hierarchy because it is the most general software quality that we would expect every software product to possess. We define *usability* as the extent to which the software is reliable, efficient, portable, and maintainable. This is illustrated in Fig. 3.2 by the subcomponents of usability. We define *reliability* as the extent to which software correctly performs its functional specifications; *efficiency* as the extent to which the software economically uses computer resources; *portability* as the extent to which the software can be operated on different computer configurations; and *maintainability* as the ease with which the software can be expanded or contracted to satisfy new requirements or can be corrected when errors or deficiencies are detected.

Since we primarily are interested in studying software maintainance, we must look more closely at the quality of maintainability. Maintainability protects software reliability by supporting testable changes and prolongs software life by supporting adaptation to new requirements and environments.[11] As shown in Fig. 3.3, a maintainable software system must possess the qualities of understandability, testability and modifiability. We define *understandability* as the extent to which we can read and understand the software code and documentation; *testability* as the ease with which we can demonstrate the correctness of software changes; *modifiability* as the ease with which we can modify the software code.

In the next section, we look at how to develop a software system possessing these quality characteristics. Unfortunately, since state-

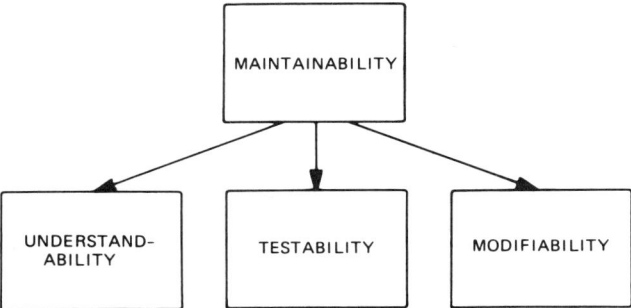

Fig. 3.3. Maintainability characteristic hierarchy.

of-the-art methods for measuring software qualities are intuitive and subjective, we can offer only guidelines to ensure software quality. For example, what is considered efficient or portable to one user, may be totally unacceptable to another. Therefore, it is extremely important to define each software quality and the criteria for measuring it in the user's terms. Then, these qualities and their measurement criteria must be conveyed to the developer and used to audit software quality as an acceptance step included in each software development phase.

3.3 SOFTWARE DEVELOPMENT PROCESS

3.3.1 Introduction

In this section, we discuss how to build maintainability into a software system. Our approach is summarized by the incorporation of the following five activities into the software development process (see Fig. 3.4):

1. Establishing the system qualities and priorities sought
2. Defining and enforcing standards
3. Documenting the software development process
4. Conducting acceptance reviews and audits
5. Including the maintainer in the development process

First, as we discussed in the previous section, the qualities sought in the software product and the priorities set by management should

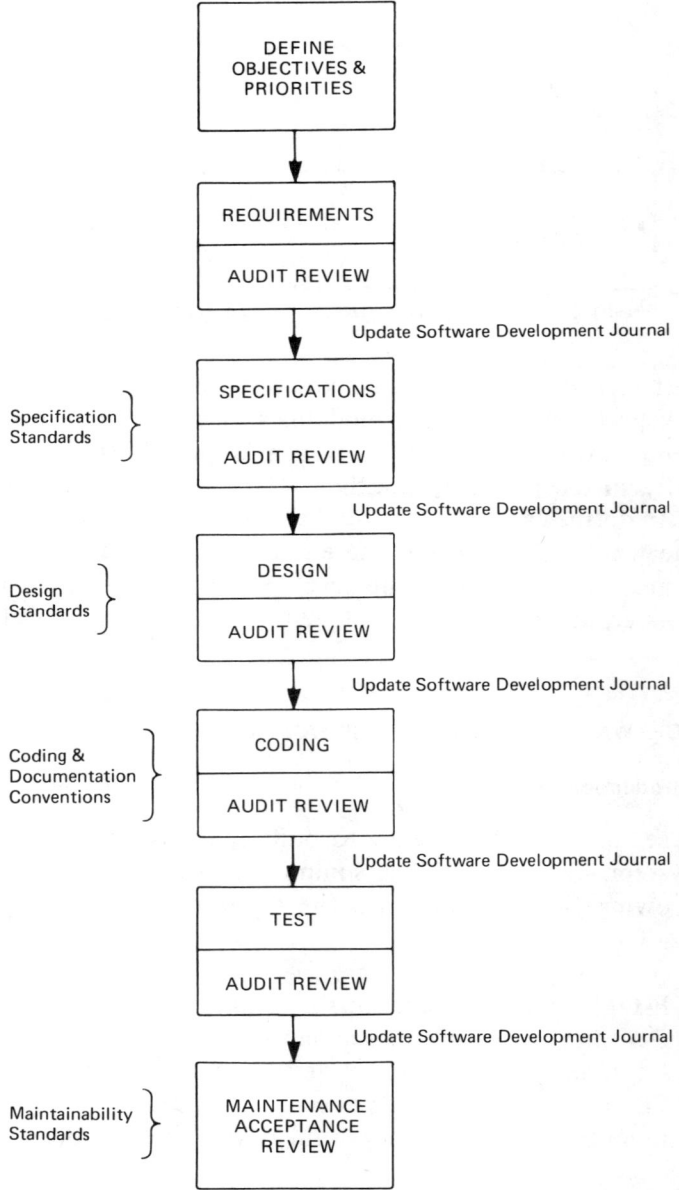

Fig. 3.4. Development phases for a maintainable software system.

be defined in writing early in the project. Clarifying project goals at project inception is the first step in building a usable software product.

Second, standards are an excellent means for assuring continuity and control throughout the software development process. Of course, standards are useless unless they are supported and enforced by management. Standards that are particularly helpful in improving software maintainability are:

1. specification standards
2. coding conventions
3. change control standards
4. documentation standards
5. quality control standards

The formality of software standards depends upon the particular needs of the developer and the user. However, once a standard is established, it should be consistently adhered to throughout the software project. If not, the benefits of introducing uniformity and completeness in a software product through standards will be lost, and the standards will be seen as a useless development constraint.

Third, in addition to documenting the software product, the software development process should be documented. The developer's objectives, priorities, basic assumptions, development philosophy, design dilemmas, algorithms, and so forth should be recorded in the System Development Journal. How the system was developed is as important as what was developed. Recording intentions, which are quickly forgotten, can greatly simplify the development and maintenance tasks.

Fourth, conducting acceptance reviews and audits at the completion of each development phase is another excellent means of controlling the software development process. This is based upon the software engineering principle:

Manage a software project using a sequential life cycle plan.[12]

Following this principle means that the next software life cycle phase does not begin until the previous phase meets the acceptance criteria. Including an audit step in each development phase will help to get the errors out early. This approach allows management to track project progress and to be informed of major problems as soon as possible; it allows the user to periodically review requirements and expectations; it allows the developer to check his interpretation of project priorities, requirements and specifications; and it allows the maintainer to perform periodic maintainability audits of the evolving software.

Finally, the maintainer should actively participate in the development process by offering suggestions, insights, tools and techniques to the developer, by requesting information necessary to provide maintenance support, and by imposing maintainability standards upon the developer. Because software systems are becoming larger and more complex, the maintainer needs time to learn about the system he must eventually support and time to prepare to support it. Waiting until the operation and maintenance phase to plan for system support greatly increases the risk of not being able to provide cost-effective support. Also, the maintainer's knowledge of the computer environment, the user, current production systems, and available packages is valuable information for the developer. Ignoring usability and maintainability issues during development has led to systems that were produced as software engineering exercises rather than as tools for user groups.

In the sections that follow, we shall expand the software engineering guidelines presented in Chapter 1. We shall present a set of guidelines intended to build the quality of maintainability into a software system.

3.3.2 Defining Requirements with Maintenance in Mind

During requirements analysis, the software system capabilities and the necessary resources are defined. This is a very difficult and very crucial phase in software development. It is difficult because the requirements must capture user needs that are often difficult to describe in technical terms. It is crucial because the quality and completeness of the requirements greatly affect the quality and completeness of the resulting software system. Poorly defined requirements can make top-down development impossible, make testing difficult, freeze out the user, destroy management control, and ultimately cause project failure.[13]

In traditional software development projects, the requirements phase has been neglected because it does not lend itself to structuring with technical tools and methodologies as does, for example, the coding phase. It is a people-oriented, more than a technical-oriented, problem. Requirements are not static; they change with time and with people. For example, during a large project, the requirements analysis phase must be performed repeatedly. As the user learns more about the system and the limits and capabilities of technology, he will refine his needs. As the developer researches possible implementation approaches, he will refine the technical resources required for the software.

Traditionally, only 10 percent of the total system effort has been spent on requirements analysis.[14] The result has been poorly understood system requirements leading to a software product that does not meet user needs and expectations. Because software systems are becoming increasingly more complex, a larger portion of the development effort is now being spent on requirements analysis.

The formality with which requirements analysis is conducted varies with the complexity of the proposed system and the structure of the development organization. At the very least, however, the following guidelines should be considered when performing requirements analysis:

1. Identify the user group.
2. Determine with the user measurable criteria for project success.
3. Justify the use of an automated system by considering project cost, development schedule constraints and the risk of project failure.
4. Determine system requirements with the user and review each requirement with the system developer.
5. Define requirements in testable terms.
6. Distinguish between hard requirements and optional requirements that can be added later.
7. Think in terms of how easily the user will be able to interact with the system.
8. Consider processing time, storage requirements, error probability, contingency development plans, chance of theft or fraud, personnel, computer time, and use of existing software when formulating requirements.

9. Write requirements in a concise form that can be clearly understood by the user and by the developer.
10. Review requirements with upper level management, discussing benefits, tradeoffs and risks involved in developing the system.
11. Require user, developer, and management acceptance approval of requirements before proceeding to the specifications phase.

Because we are primarily interested in development from the maintainer's viewpoint, we expand the requirements analysis guidelines to ensure the software quality of maintainability:

1. Identify the user group *and* the maintenance group.
2. Review each system requirement with the system developer *and* the system maintainer.
3. Consider this system's impact on existing operational systems.
4. Consider the operation and maintenance support effort when formulating requirements.
5. Determine proposed priorities, enhancement schedules, and manpower and computer resources needed for implementing the optional requirements.
6. Determine what capabilities and facilities are likely to change and are needed to maintain different versions of the system.
7. Identify requirement subsets to allow for system contractions and expansions.
8. Examine the feasibility of expanding critical resources after system development.

Notice that in the above guidelines, the system maintainer is involved in the requirements analysis phase. This is necessary to determine a realistic picture of software system capabilities and resources needed over its entire life cycle. Also, it allows the maintainer to plan for the support of the new system with personnel and computer facility preparations (see Fig. 3.5).

3.3.3 Defining Specifications with Maintenance in Mind

System specifications describe how system requirements are to be met. Specifications include definitions for input/output formats,

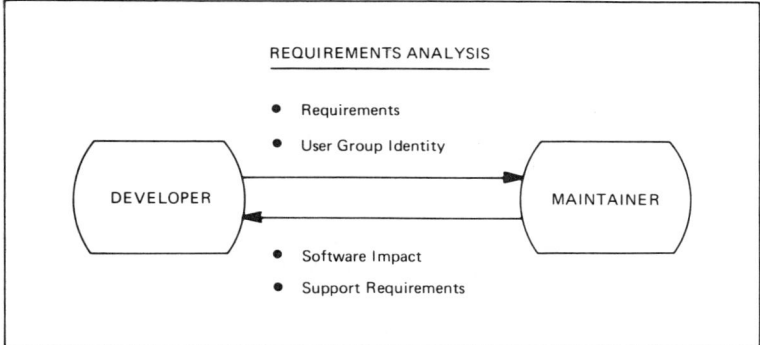

Fig. 3.5. Requirements analysis phase: information exchange between system developer and maintainer.

data structures, data bases, external files, internal tables, functional components, and interfaces with other systems. They offer to the user and to the developer a concrete description of the system functions, to avoid confusion on the user's part and errors on the developer's part. The specification phase is extremely important because the completeness and the correctness of the specifications affect the success of the entire software development project. Specifications are used to develop project schedules, manpower assignments, test plans, and user documentation. If the specifications are incomplete or incorrect, they can cause schedule delays, inadequate testing, and incorrect user documentation. A software system derived from poor specifications cannot be expected to be reliable or useful.

The specification phase is another phase that has been neglected in traditional software development. Because programmers have been anxious to begin coding and project managers have been anxious to show tangible results of progress to management and to the user, only 10 percent of the total system development effort is normally spent defining specifications.[15] This has had an adverse effect on system reliability.

With the advent of structured programming, attention is shifting to the development phases that precede coding and testing. Formality, such as management reviews, and technical tools, such as automated specification languages, have been introduced to structure the specification phase. Some general guidelines suggested for structuring the specification phase are:

1. Base specification definition upon system requirements to ensure that the system will meet user needs.
2. Develop specification document standards to ensure readability and completeness.
3. Describe specifications in terms that are testable and include test methods as part of the specification document.
4. Review specifications with management and with the user periodically to ensure their correctness and completeness.
5. Include in the specification document suggestions for the design approach, programming languages, and the order in which system components should be developed.
6. Identify existing systems/modules/packages to be used as building blocks in development.
7. Require user, developer and management acceptance approval of the specifications before proceeding to the design phase.

To these guidelines, four maintainability guidelines are added:

1. Identify subsets of functional and data structure components that are initially required and those that are optionally needed in the base system.
2. Review specifications with the user, developer, *and* maintainer.
3. Evaluate with the maintainer packages and existing systems/modules as possible candidate components to be used in system development.
4. Examine with the maintainer the impact on existing software systems and computer operations environment.

Again, notice that the maintainer is included in system development. Not only is he given the opportunity to become familiar with the software system he must eventually support, but also he actively contributes to its development by suggesting components to be used in building the new system and approaches to use in testing it. His knowledge of existing systems and packages can save the developer

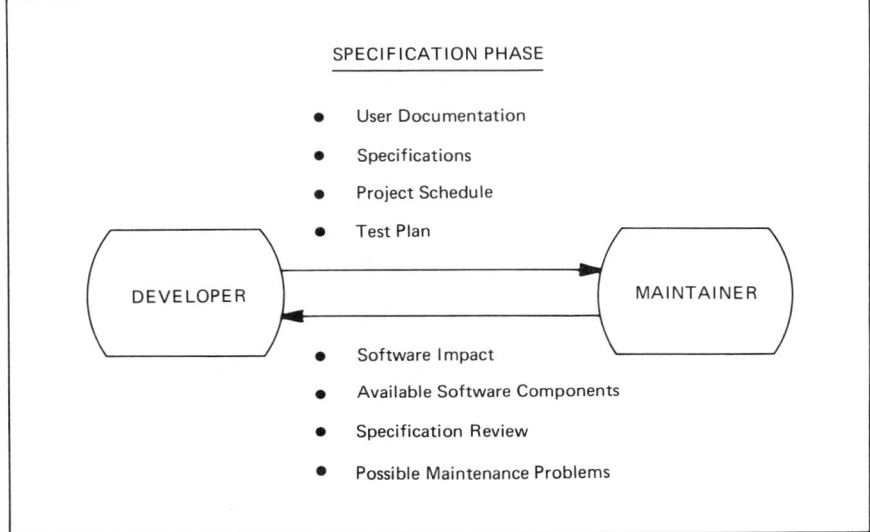

Fig. 3.6. Specification phase: information exchange between system developer and maintainer.

from "reinventing the wheel." Using existing components that have already been tested and have demonstrated reliability can improve system reliability and reduce development time (see Fig. 3.6).

3.3.4 Designing with Maintenance in Mind

In large projects, requirements and design errors often exceed coding errors. In a TRW study of errors detected during or after acceptance test, design errors outweighed coding errors 64 percent to 36 percent.[16] Not only do more design errors occur, but also they are more costly to correct than coding errors. Design errors require more time to diagnose and more time to correct than coding errors. In a study by Shooman,[17] it was determined that correcting a design error during coding is twice the effort of correcting it during design and correcting it during testing is ten times the effort of correcting it during the design. In other words, most errors are design errors and the earlier a design error is detected and corrected during software development, the less costly it is to correct.

Many advances have been made in the development of methodologies and tools for improving the design process. The collection of state-of-the-art design methodologies is commonly referred to as structured design. The objectives of structured design are:

1. to systematize the design process
2. to produce a hierarchical design description that can be implemented as a well-structured program
3. to offer a framework in which problem solving can proceed effectively

The structured design approach is an extension of the modularization principle. In modularization, the system is divided into pieces called modules. In a structured design, the system modules are arranged in a conceptual hierarchy representing a set of functions that the software system must perform to fulfill specification requirements. The suggested method of arriving at a structured design is by step-wise refinement. This is the process of dividing the design phase into steps. At each step a design decision concerning the definition of a system function or a data structure is made. To ensure the correctness of the design, it is important that at each design step only one, simple decision is made and that the process of decision-making as well as the decision is recorded.

A structured design is guided by one of two design approaches:

1. Top-down approach
2. Bottom-up approach [18]

The top-down approach employs a step-wise refinement philosophy that builds the design by dividing system functions into subfunctions (see Fig. 3.7). In simple design steps, the functional and data structure components of the system are defined in greater and greater detail. The bottom-up approach follows the opposite design principle. It builds the system design by combining simple functions to form more complex functions. The top-down approach is preferred when the designer is sure that feasible low level functions (e.g., operating system interface routines) can be constructed to fulfill system requirements. It is also preferred when decisions concerning data

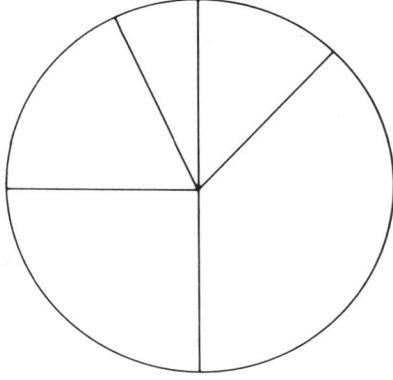

- DIVIDE BIG PROBLEM INTO EASIER TO SOLVE SMALLER PROBLEMS

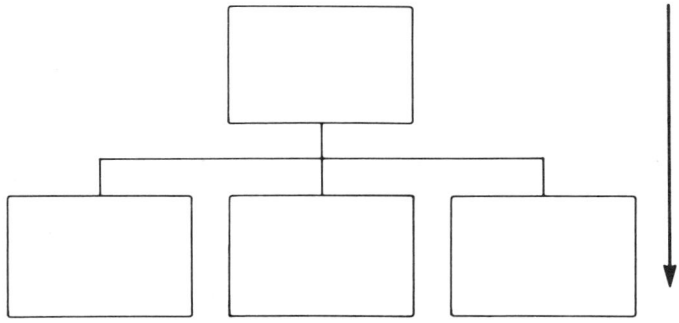

- PRODUCE A HIERARCHY OF PROGRAM COMPONENTS
- START AT TOP COMPONENT AND PROCEED DOWN THE HIERARCHY

Fig. 3.7. Top-down design approach.

structures (e.g., file access methods) must be delayed. The bottom-up approach is preferred when the sytem is a generalization or extension of an existing system. In this case, using previously coded and tested library routines can simplify software development.

Following a pure top-down or pure bottom-up approach can cause design errors. For example, when following a top-down approach, common functions may not be recognized, or a top-down design may require too much time for a large software system. On the other hand, following a pure bottom-up approach can result in poorly designed module interfaces making integration testing impossible.

Of the two, the top-down approach is usually considered the more useful. But how useful either approach is ultimately depends upon the skills of the designer, the computing facilities available, and the particulars of the system. No design approach can answer specific design questions for an arbitrary software system. It can only guide development by outlining the design procedure. The designer must fill in the detail by making each design decision and by choosing the best design alternative. In practice, the design process is usually a combination top-down/bottom-up, iterative process. During each design iteration, the designer evaluates the design in terms of its implementation feasibility and the user needs and priorities. Are there technical tools (e.g., operating systems, language compilers, editors, debugging aids, libraries) and the computing facilities (e.g., hardware configurations, operations personnel) available to implement this design within the schedule and cost constraints? The designer must review the proposed design with management and with the user to ensure a correct interpretation of the system specifications.

In traditional software development projects, only 15 percent of the total project effort is spent on the design phase.[19] At least 50 percent of the project effort should be spent on defining requirements, specifications, and the design. The success of the coding and testing phases depends directly upon the quality and completeness of the design. Although the design of software is a creative, problem-solving activity, the design process should be structured and should be comprised of the following elements:

1. Researching—
   Technical tools, programming algorithms, and existing software components should be examined in researching the optimum design solution.
2. Step-wise Decision Making—
   The design process should be structured in simple design decision steps that examine alternate design solutions.

3. Recording—
   Both the design solution and the design decision-making strategy should be recorded.
4. Reviewing—
   The components of the design solution should be reviewed several times during the design process with the developer to ensure correctness, with the user to ensure completeness and with the mangement to ensure project visibility.

Also, the guidelines listed below should be followed to structure the design phase:

1. There should be an element of top-down and bottom-up in every design. The designer should keep in mind an overview of the entire solution and also the facilities and capabilities of the computing environment.
2. The design should proceed in explicit steps. As little as possible should be decided at each step, and attempts should be made to make the easiest decisions first. Decisions concerning data structures should be deferred as long as possible to avoid eliminating alternative designs prematurely. Design decisions should be guided by criteria such as efficiency, storage economy, clarity, and consistency of design.
3. Design alternatives should be investigated to find the optimum design solution.
4. The designer should strive for design simplicity.
5. The system should be divided into conceptually understandable modules. The modules should be arranged in a hierarchical order dictating how modules can be invoked and how they interact with one another.
6. Design integrity should be preserved by defining a system philosophy and following it.
7. Off-nominal inputs, error detection, and recovery should be considered in the design.
8. The design process and the design should be documented with the use of structure charts, HIPO diagrams, pseudo-code, and Chapin charts.

50 PART 2 MANAGING SOFTWARE DEVELOPMENT

9. Acceptance approval of the design should be required from the user, developer, and management before proceeding to the coding phase.

The system maintainer should be involved in the design phase. During the requirements and specifications phases, he learned the general system objectives and requirements that enabled him to begin preparations of personnel, equipment and tools needed to support the system. The design phase provides more detailed information about the system, allowing continued support preparations. However, he cannot simply be a recipient of information; he also should actively contribute to the design. As maintainer, he has information crucial to the resolution of an optimum design solution (see Fig. 3.8).

First, the maintainer is familiar with the capabilities and limitations of the computing facility. Although the designer should not allow current limitations to prematurely narrow the design alternatives considered, he must be aware of practical limitations in arriving

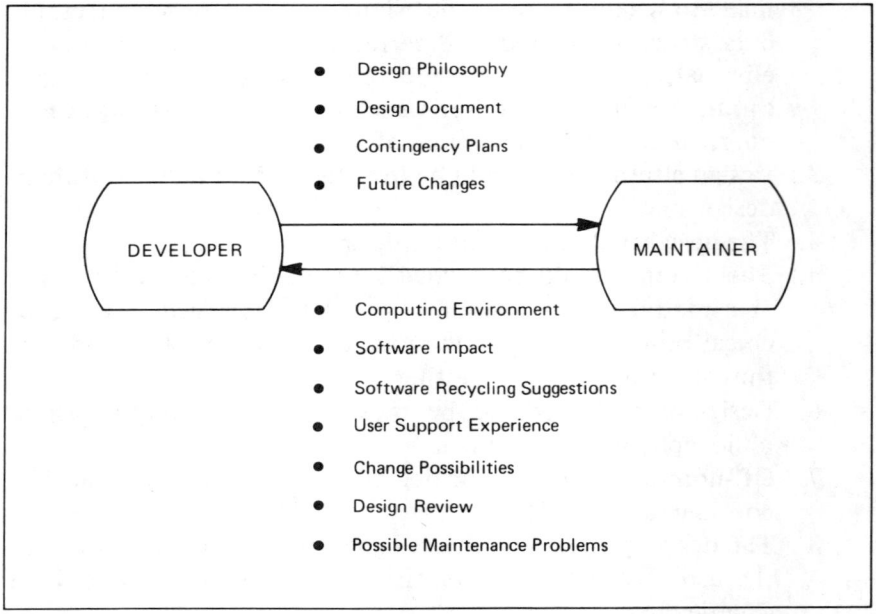

Fig. 3.8. Design phase: information exchange between system developer and maintainer

at a feasible design. Also, the maintainer has extensive knowledge of the operations requirements of existing production systems. The impact of introducing this system into an existing production system environment must be investigated as part of the design.

Second, the maintainer is familiar with the common routine libraries and existing production systems that perform functions similar to those requested in the new system. The existence of such routines and systems should be brought to the designer's attention because "software recycling" can reduce system development time and improve system reliability.[20]

Third, the maintainer may have previous experience with the user through the support of production systems. This experience may offer insights into the user's needs, priorities, level of technical sophistication, and change requirements. These insights should be considered by the designer in attempting to design a well-engineered and easily modifiable system.

Fourth, the ability to change is a critical part of system maintainability. Based on previous experiences in handling changes due to error correction, environment changes and user requests, the maintainer can suggest typical ways in which a system can be expected to change. Examining changes that occurred in previous systems may help the designer build into the design a more realistic flexibility than arbitrarily placed stubs for future growth. Also, considering change possibilities may help the designer evaluate the degree of generality versus flexibility to be designed into the system. Generality allows a system to be used for a variety of changing functions without introducing modifications, while flexibility allows a system to be modified easily.[21] An optimum design includes the appropriate degree of each to most effectively meet the user's changing needs and to prepare for contingency planning. In the event of development problems, a flexible design can be modified to accommodate a more modest version of the system that can be developed within the original scheduling and cost constraints.

To ensure the quality of maintainability, some additional design guidelines are suggested:

1. Design for flexibility to extend, contract, and change the system.

2. Study possible future changes with the designer, user, and maintainer.
3. Perform change exercises on the design to test its flexibility.
4. Investigate software recycling with the maintainer.
5. Include the maintainer in design reviews to react to design implementation feasibility, effect on existing systems, and human engineering factors.
6. Evaluate the generality of the system design in terms of its ability to:[22]
    a. execute on different hardware configurations.
    b. operate on different input/output formats.
    c. function in "subset mode" performing a selected set of features.
    d. operate with different data structures or algorithms depending upon resource availability.
7. Evaluate the flexibility of the system design in terms of its ability to:[23]
    a. isolate specialized functions that are likely to change in separate modules.
    b. provide module interfaces that are insensitive to expected changes.
    c. identify a subset of the system that can be made operational as part of contingency planning.
8. Achieve greater flexibility by allowing each module to perform one unique function.

3.3.5 Coding with Maintenance in Mind

The coding phase has been mastered better than any other software life cycle phase. Structured programming has taken much of the mystique out of programming, replacing it with discipline, standardization, and control. The objective of structured programming (as a means of structuring code) is to produce a well-structured program that is reliable, readable, and maintainable. The methods for achieving this objective include:

1. Standardization of the program instruction set
2. Limitation of the use of program control structures

DEVELOPING SOFTWARE WITH MAINTENANCE IN MIND 53

3. Definition of the characteristics of a module and module interaction
4. Restriction of the flow of program control to a simple scheme where control is passed from one level to the next *and* then back
5. Imposition of a set of documentation conventions

Benefits reported from employing structured programming fall into four categories:

1. Readability
2. Reliability
3. Productivity
4. Maintainability

There have been many results reported to substantiate these benefits.

In the SMCS project discussed in Chapter 2, programmers believed that the standardization of style introduced by structured programming conventions made the program easier to read. IBM studies report an average savings of 40 percent because of increased programmer productivity.[24] In traditional programming efforts that did not employ structured programming, the average programmer productivity rate was 5 to 10 source statements per programmer per day. As shown in Fig. 3.9, several efforts that did employ structured programming reported a programmer productivity rate of 17 to 65 statements per programmer per day.[25] In many efforts that employed structured programming, less time was spent in the testing phase because fewer test runs were required to reach an operational state. The maintenance effort of structured software is reported to be less than for unstructured systems. As shown in Fig. 3.10, the average error frequency rate in tested unstructured software is 50 errors per 10,000 lines of code, but in several structured software systems it has been reduced to 0 to 5 errors per 10,000 lines of code.[26]

Although structured programming has been shown to improve software, its use cannot guarantee reduced software costs or increased software maintainability. Some common problems associated with structured programming are:

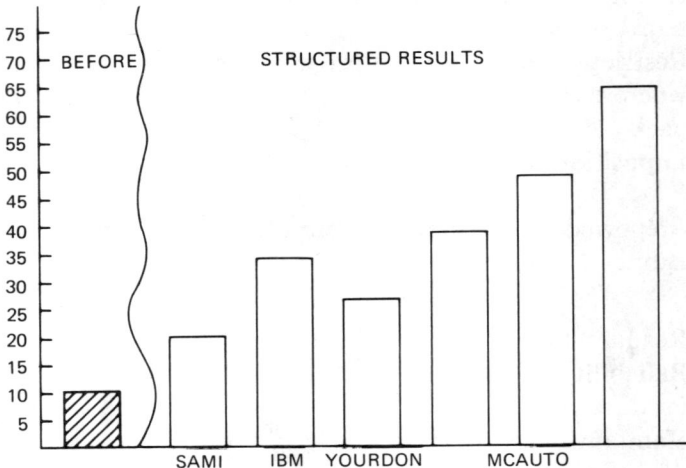

Fig. 3.9. Programmer productivity improvements with structured programming.

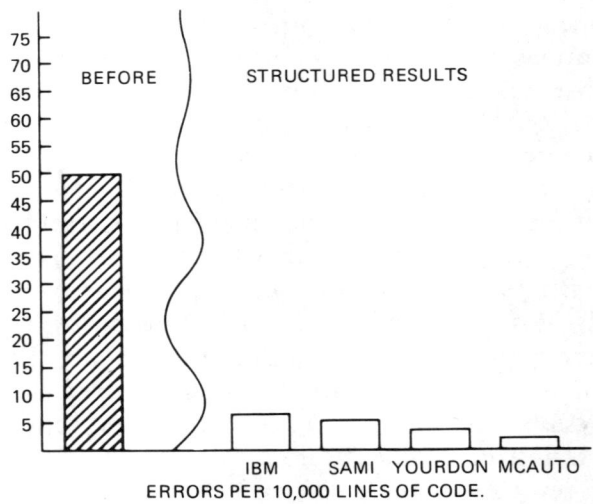

ERRORS PER 10,000 LINES OF CODE.

Fig. 3.10. Software maintenance improvements with structured programming.

DEVELOPING SOFTWARE WITH MAINTENANCE IN MIND 55

1. Expecting too much in terms of reduced development time and reduced development costs
2. Ignoring coding standards and other management controls
3. Encouraging structuring purism that can introduce inefficiencies and inflexibility
4. Eliminating periodic project reviews
5. Ignoring the user
6. Using structured programming as a substitute for problem-solving and management skills

In spite of the above problems, structured programming should be used to guide the coding phase and, in addition, the following guidelines should be used:

1. Use state-of-the-art tools such as well-engineered operating systems, reliable and efficient compilers, packages, structuring preprocessors, cross-reference generators, documentation generators, software management library systems, and source code analyzers.
2. Use high-level programming languages where feasible.
3. Use only standard versions and features of a programming language.
4. Document source code to explain the function that each module is to perform and choose descriptive data and procedure names.
5. Isolate machine interfaces into special interface modules to allow for hardware and operating system flexibility.
6. Limit the number of files each module accesses.
7. Avoid self-modifying code and hard-coded parameters.
8. Define module intercommunication based upon the function the modules perform, not upon how the modules work internally.

Are there any additional coding guidelines to improve software maintainability? Code that is easy to maintain should be readable, reliable, and should comply with coding standards. To ensure maintainability in this respect, consider the following guidelines (see Fig. 3.11):

56 PART 2 MANAGING SOFTWARE DEVELOPMENT

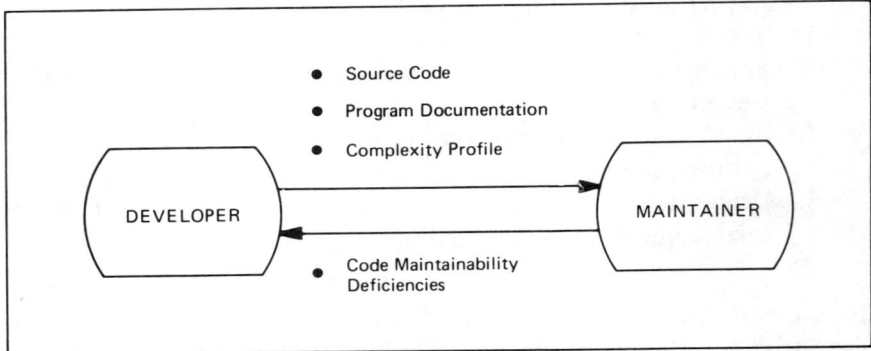

Fig. 3.11. Coding phase: information exchange between system developer and maintainer.

1. The source code should be inspected prior to the testing phase by someone other than the original coder to audit compliance to specifications and to standards.
2. Complexity analysis of the source code should be performed to measure understandability.

The first guideline promotes the writing of error-free code. Studies by Myers have shown that the programmer often is not the best person to review his code.[27] Because of personal attachment and because of familiarity, a programmer often reads his code the way he thinks it is written rather than the way it is actually written. An impartial reader can find errors and standards violations that are not obvious to the coder. Myers' study also pointed out that different people find different errors. Having more people read the code is likely to reveal more errors before the testing phase begins, thus simplifying testing and reducing overall development costs. Because programmers are likely to focus more attention on normal processing and on internal logic, the code inspector should concentrate on error handling and input/output processing as well as checking compliance to specifications and standards.

The second guideline promotes code readability. The term complexity is used in the sense of psychological complexity. The more complex a software system, the more difficult it is to read and to understand. Obviously, the system maintainer is interested in readability. If he cannot read and understand the code, he cannot effectively maintain it.

Complexity is a measure of the degree of decision-making present in a piece of code. It is a function of the number of possible execution paths and the control structures and control variables used to direct path selection. Since one-third of the statements in an average program are concerned with the flow of control, complexity is a significant factor in predicting software development and maintenance costs.[28]

Because it imposes restrictions on program structure and style, structured programming is a suggested means of controlling program complexity. However, even a well-structured program can be very difficult to understand because of its size, the number of modules that interact, the number of variables used to direct path selection, and the number and types of functions that are performed. Therefore, an additional means for controlling complexity should be employed as a post-step to the coding phase.

The source code should be examined to determine its complexity. Not only should the complexity of the entire system be measured, but also the complexity of each module. Modules that are especially complex should be identified, since these portions of the system will be more difficult to maintain. Such information is necessary for establishing usability, testability, and maintainability acceptance criteria. The developer should be encouraged to redesign and recode portions of the system that are extremely complex relative to the rest of the system.

One measure of complexity has not been agreed upon, but several guidelines have been suggested:

1. Limit the size of a module to 50 statements (instructions).[29]
2. Limit the number of compares per module to 10.[30]
3. Minimize the complexity of each module and evenly distribute complexity among modules.[31]
4. Localize the use of variables as much as possible.
5. Identify common modules and how they are invoked.

Table 3.1. Complexity Profile

- Size of Program (Number of statements or instructions)
- Number of Modules in Program
- Number of Variables in Program
- Number of Global Variables in Program
- Average Module Size (In statements)
- Average Number of Compares per Module
- Average Number of Modules Accessing a Global Variable
- List of Common Modules
- List of Modules that Access More than the Average Number of Global Variables
- List of Modules that Exceed the Module Size Limit of 50 Statements or Exceed the Module Compare Limit of 10 Compares

A Complexity Profile of each program should be constructed with the information shown in Table 3.1. The Complexity Profile can be used by the developer to identify complex modules which should be redesigned or, at the very least, tested most thoroughly. During the testing phase, the developer can compare the complexity information with test results to evaluate the validity of the complexity measure. (The assumption is that more complex modules are more difficult to test.) Also, the Complexity Profile can be used by the maintainer to identify modules that may be difficult to understand and to modify.

3.3.6 Testing with Maintenance in Mind

Testing is one of the most important phases of software development. It is the process of guaranteeing that a program works in all cases in which it is supposed to work. If a program were executed with every possible test case, then it could be guaranteed to work correctly. But for most programs this degree of testing is impossible due to time and cost constraints. Instead, the correctness of a program is assured by testing it with a small sample of carefully chosen test cases. The tester's task is to use the specifications along with sound testing principles and a knowledge of the internal program structure to eliminate unexpected program conditions and failures and to discover any incorrect implementation of the specifications.

Thoroughness of testing is guided by the following rules:[32]

1. Every program statement and every path should be executed at least once.
2. The most heavily used parts of the program should be tested most thoroughly.
3. All modules should be tested individually before they are combined. Then, the paths and intersections between the modules should be tested.
4. Testing should proceed from the simplest to the most complex test cases; that is, tests involving fewer loops and conditions should be performed before tests involving more complicated logic.
5. Test cases should be developed by more than one group to exercise the logic more thoroughly.

Traditionally, the test phase is divided into a four step procedure:

1. Unit testing
2. Integration testing
3. System testing
4. Acceptance testing

Unit testing is performed for each module in a program. The objective of unit testing are to execute each statement in the module, to traverse each logic path in the module, and to test the module with each possible set of input data. A comprehensive unit test minimally should include the following components:

1. All logic paths in a module should be exercised once.
2. All valid transaction types should be tested to assure that valid results will be produced.
3. Some invalid data transactions or test elements should be tested to assure that appropriate error messages and error processing are performed.

Unit testing steps should:

1. "Walk through" the code to determine if the specifications are correctly implemented.
2. Execute the simplest possible test to verify the basic structure of the module.
3. Examine the module performance on valid input data.
4. Examine the module performance on invalid input data.
5. Examine the correctness of each loop, and especially check for proper loop termination.

Unit testing is usually the responsibility of the programmer who coded the module.

Integration testing is performed after a module is unit tested. The objectives of integration testing are to verify that a module functions correctly in its program environment and to verify that modules interact correctly. Integration testing is performed by combining modules in steps. At each step, a module is added to the program environment, and the testing concentrates on exercising the newly added module. Sometimes regression testing is included as a second component of integration testing. In regression testing, tests exercise the other modules in the program to determine if they have been adversely affected by the new module. When it has been demonstrated that a module functions properly in its environment, another module is added and integration testing continues. This process is repeated until all modules have been integrated and tested.

There are two approaches to integration testing:

1. Bottom-up testing
2. Top-down testing

In bottom-up testing, the lowest-level modules are integrated and tested first. The bottom-up approach requires the construction of driver programs to simulate the program environment during integration testing. Several problems have been noted with bottom-up testing:[33]

1. Driver programs can require a great deal of effort to develop and can be an additional source of errors.

DEVELOPING SOFTWARE WITH MAINTENANCE IN MIND

   2. High-level specifications and design are tested last and least.
   3. Interface errors may not appear until late in integration testing.

In top-down testing, high-level modules are integrated and tested first. Each module is tested by representing the lower-level modules as stubs. As testing progresses, each stub is replaced by the module code. The advantages of top-down testing include:

   1. The test data needed grows as integration testing proceeds, allowing for pooling of test data instead of requiring separate test data for each module as it is integrated.
   2. High-level design components are tested first and are tested most.
   3. Integration testing can be begun earlier since high-level modules can be coded first and can be tested with stubs.

Problems noted with top-down testing are:

   1. Module stubs can be as difficult to construct as coding the actual module.
   2. Planned modules, which are represented as stubs, may not be discovered to be infeasible to code or to test until late in the project.

In small programs, it makes little difference which integration approach is used. In large systems, a combination top-down/bottom-up approach is often preferred. A top-down approach is used that incorporates the advantages of the bottom-up approach by dealing first with the most complex, critical parts of the system.

Some general integration testing guidelines are:

   1. Use the top-down approach to test the basic program structure verifying the correctness of the high level design as soon as possible.
   2. Use the bottom-up approach to test modules that interface with the operating system in complex or new ways as soon as possible.

62   PART 2 MANAGING SOFTWARE DEVELOPMENT

3. Include regression testing as a component of integration testing.

System testing is performed following successful completion of integration testing. The objective of system testing is to discover any incorrect implementation of the specifications. Typical strategies for system testing include:

1. Test cases which exercise the most important and most heavily used parts of the system.
2. Test cases which represent normal or expected use of the system.
3. Test cases which are selected to expose errors under extreme or critical processing conditions.

A comprehensive system test should include tests to cover each of the above strategies. Guidelines for system testing are:

1. The program functional requirements and specifications should be used to build test cases.
2. Test cases should include expected test results.
3. Testing should begin with the simplest tests and graduate to the more complex tests, first using constructed and then using actual test data.
4. System testing should include three types of test cases:
   a. Normal Cases—Show that the program produces correct results for expected input data.
   b. Extreme Cases—Test extremes in input volume as well as input values.
   c. Exception Cases—Use test data that falls out of the acceptable range to show that the program explicitly rejects all invalid input data.
5. When possible, run in parallel with a predesessor system and compare results.

In *acceptance testing*, the program is treated as a black box. No knowledge of the internal structure is assumed, since testing is completely based upon the specifications. Acceptance testing is performed after system testing is completed and involves the user. Using

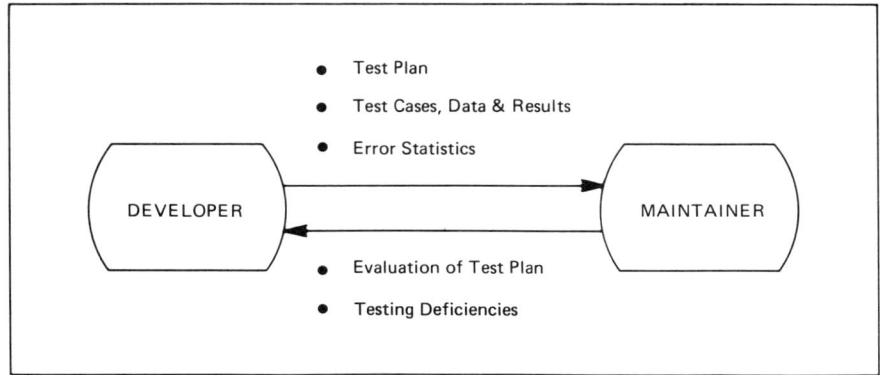

Fig. 3.12. Testing phase: information exchange between system developer and maintainer.

simulated operations, the program is examined under normal, stressed, and degraded conditions. The total software package is checked out. Also, information regarding performance efficiencies and limitations is recorded.

The system maintainer is interested in the testing phase as a recipient of information and as a participant in testing. First, since the system will be repeatedly retested during the maintenance phase, the maintainer should have copies of the test plan, the test data, and the test case results produced during the development phases (see Fig. 3.12). When the system is modified, it can be retested with these test cases and the results can be compared. Also, the maintainer should receive information on the number and types of errors found during development. In the past, this information has not been recorded. However, since there may be a correlation between the number of errors detected during development and system reliability,[34] error information should become part of the permanent system documentation. Systems that are difficult to test are often difficult to maintain. Also, error information can be useful in pinpointing portions of the system that are error-prone and difficult to modify. A Test History of each program tested should be compiled with the information shown in Table 3.2.

Second, the system maintainer should actively participate in the testing. When the test plan is developed, it should be reviewed by the maintainer. Using his objectivity, his experience with supporting

Table 3.2. Program Test History.

Unit Test History

- Number of Modules Unit Tested
- Average Number of Unit Tests Executed per Module
- Number of Errors Discovered during Testing
- Average Number of Errors Discovered in a Module (UAEM)
- Total Number of Statements Modified to Correct Errors
- List of Modules in which the Number of Errors Discovered Exceeds UAEM
- Types of Errors Discovered
  − Hardware Failure
  − Software Reaction to Hardware Failure
  − Coding Error
  − Design Error
  − Specification Error
- Average Length of Time to Discover and Correct an Error

Integration Test History

- Number of Integration Tests Executed
- Number of Errors Discovered during Integration Testing
- Average Number of Errors Discovered in a Module (IAEM)
- List of Modules in which the Number of Errors Discovered Exceeds IAEM
- Total Number of Statements Modified to Correct Errors
- Total Number of Modules Modified to Correct Errors
- Types of Errors Discovered
- Average Length of Time to Discover and to Correct an Error

System (Acceptance) Test History

- Number of System (Acceptance) Tests Executed
- Number of Errors Discovered during System (Acceptance) Testing
- Average Number of Errors Discovered per Module (SAEM)
- List of Modules Modified to Correct Errors
- Number of Statements Modified to Correct Errors
- Types of Errors Discovered
- Average Length of Time to Correct an Error

Complexity Correlation Figures

- List of Modules whose Complexity Exceeds the Complexity Limits and UAEM or IAEM or SAEM
- List of Modules whose Complexity Exceeds the Complexity Limits and which was Modified to Correct a System (Acceptance) Error

systems, and his interpretation of the system specifications, the maintainer should evaluate the completeness of the test plan. A comprehensive test plan should be available during the design phase and should contain:

1. Testing objectives
2. Testing philosophies/approaches
3. Test tools
4. Test data and expected results
5. Testing, problem reporting, error correction and retesting procedures
6. Testing acceptance criteria

Further, the maintainer should participate in the testing procedures. According to Myers, a programmer is relatively unsuccessful in testing his own program. For example, most changes made to a program during unit testing are style rather than error-correction changes. Also, testing done by independent groups is likely to detect more and different errors than when all testing is done by only one group or one individual.[35] To introduce objectivity, testing should be conducted by a group other than the developer, such as a quality assurance group or the maintenance group. Since the maintainer has a selfish interest in ensuring system reliability and in gaining system familiarity, his involvement in the test phase should be encouraged.

3.3.7 Maintainability Standards

In our presentation of maintainability guidelines for software development, we have stressed the need for active participation of the maintainer in each development phase. Establishing a communication channel between the software development group and the maintenance group allows the exchange of information necessary for ensuring the software quality of maintainability. Figure 3.13 summarizes the types of information exchanged.

During the software development process, the maintainer must define for the developer maintainability standards to be used as maintenance acceptance criteria at project completion. Formalizing what is needed to support a software system will enable the developer to

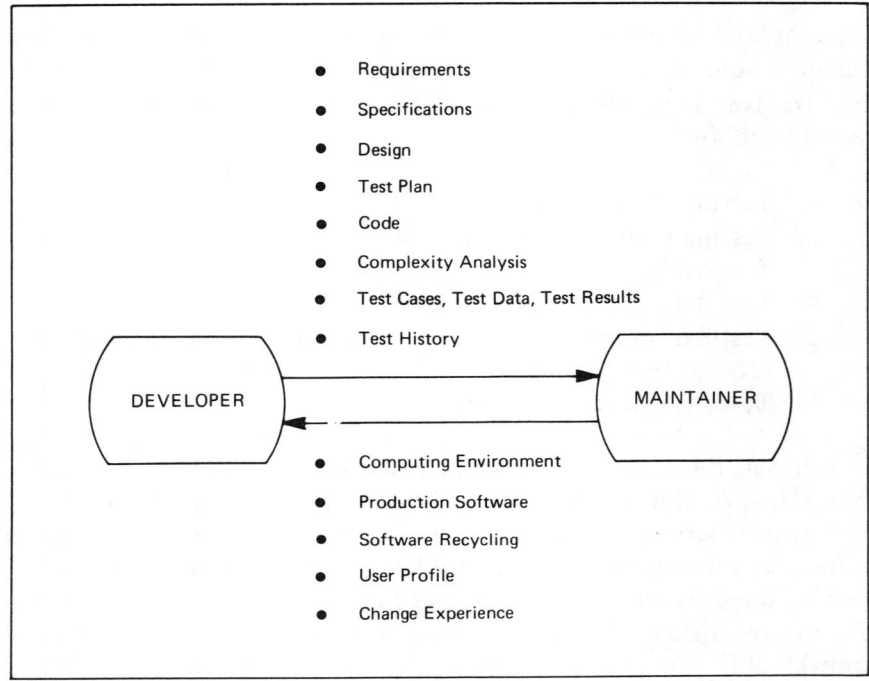

Fig. 3.13. Software developer–maintainer information exchange.

prepare the appropriate information and material for the maintenance phase. A software system will not be accepted by the maintainer for support unless it meets all of the maintenance criteria.

Maintainability standards should include the following:

1. Requirements
   - Requirements should be written, prioritized, and defined in testable terms.
   - Required, optional, and future requirements should be differentiated.
   - Requirements should include computing facility requirements for operations and for maintenance testing, operational and maintenance personnel requirements, and support and test tools.

2. Specifications
    - Specifications should be written and defined in testable terms.
    - Required, optional, and future functions should be differenciated.
3. Design
    - Extensibility, contractability, and adaptability capabilities of the design should be explained with examples and exercises of expected changes.
4. Source Code
    - High-level languages should be used whenever possible.
    - Only standard versions and standard features of programming languages should be allowed.
    - All code should be well-structured.
    - All code should be documented to explain the purpose of each module, its inputs, its outputs, and its variables to faciliate module testing.
5. System Information
    - All system documents should be made available to the system maintainer as soon as possible after their definition. These include:
        - Requirements
        - Functional specifications
        - Design documents
        - Test plan, test cases, test data and anticipated test results
        - User manuals
    - System documentation explaining system inputs and outputs, methods/algorithms used, error recovery procedures, all parameter ranges, and the default conditions should be included.
    - The System Development Journal should be given to the system maintainer at project completion. It includes:
        - Project objectives
        - Project priorities
        - Basic assumptions
        - Development philosophies
        - Design dilemmas and trade-offs

- Change requirements
- System problem areas and weak points
* A copy of the Complexity Profile should be given to the system maintainer for inspection as a post-coding step.
* A copy of the Test History should be given to the system maintainer when the Testing Phase is completed.

3.4 SUMMARY

In this chapter, we expanded upon the guideline: Develop software with maintenance in mind. Our approach included the following:

* Establish standards for development procedures and system documents.
* Use the structured programming methodology.
* Record the development process explaining the development philosophy and the decision-making process.
* Strive for simplicity.
* Study possible future changes and enhancements.
* Measure the complexity of system components.
* Record system weak points and trouble spots.
* Record the error history from the development testing phase.
* Establish acceptance criteria to evaluate software quality, with particular attention to the quality of maintainability.

Our approach stressed the active involvement of the maintainer in the development life cycle phases:

1. Requirements Analysis. The requirements analysis is the maintainer's first exposure to the system. During the requirements phase, the maintainer reviews the requirements and the resources necessary to support the proposed system as an operational system. The maintainer also evaluates the impact of this system upon existing systems.
2. Specifications. During the specification phase, the maintainer continues preparations to support the new system, in addition

to discussing with the developer the possibility of utilizing existing software components in the construction of the new system.
3. Design. The maintainer participates in the design phase by evaluating the design feasibility in terms of the resources needed for implementation and operation, human engineering, software recycling, and the flexibility to handle changes and contingency plans.
4. Coding. During the coding phase, the maintainer analyzes the complexity of the code to measure its readability and to identify pockets of complexity in the code that could cause future maintenance problems.
5. Testing. The maintainer participates in integration, system, and acceptance testing by independently conducting independent tests based upon the system specifications. Also, the developer and the maintainer gather error statistics on the numbers and types of errors discovered during development. This information is used by the maintainer to determine which portions of the system are more error-prone and therefore more difficult to maintain.

Organizing the Software Development Team

4.1 INTRODUCTION

The "one-man-programming-band" concept is no longer considered a feasible approach for most software development projects. Over the years, the typical software project has grown in magnitude, duration, complexity, and impact on the organization it serves. Because many man-years of effort are often required to complete a project, a software team must be assembled. Besides the technical problems we encounter in producing complex, multi-function, critical systems, there is great difficulty in organizing and managing the software development team. This arises in part from management inexperience in handling the data processing function and in part from insufficient project organization structures and controls.

Management considers programmers different and separate from other professionals in the organization. Management believes that because of its analytical, yet creative nature, programming cannot be controlled in the same manner as other production processes. The software product, although often essential to the existence and wellbeing of the organization, is understood by only a few trained, technical minds. The mystique, the necessity, and the status surrounding computers in the eyes of management encompasses both the machine and the people who program it. Programmers are viewed as sensitive technicians who must work alone undisturbed by management and by the user and who must not be expected to unveil the product until it is completely finished. Programmers have capitalized upon management fear and inexperience with computers and have raised themselves to *prima donna* level in many organizations.

The mystique surrounding programming—coupled with a poorly defined project organization—makes project management a formidable, if not impossible, task. Because the evolving software product is virtually invisible to management and to the user, it cannot be evaluated until completion. Because responsibilities are not clearly defined among the various team members, project progress cannot be monitored and controlled by management. As pointed out in Chapter 2, this lack of management direction and control has contributed to the failure of many software development projects.

Software projects must be structured and must be subjected to management attention and controls. Programmers must be drawn into the total organization. They must be recognized by management as part of the organization and as bounded by the organizational structure. They must receive direction and feedback from management to understand the role they play in the success and survival of the total organization. They must appreciate their product as a tool contributing to the well-being of the organization as well as an exercise in problem-solving and programming. They must be provided with growth paths and opportunities, a set of priorities, and a system of rewards and punishments within the organization.

The software product must be made visible and understandable to management so its development progress can be monitored. The organization of the development team must be formalized so that priorities and assignments are clearly understood by the team and by management.

The organization of the team is important not only because it can make management controls possible, but also because it has a direct influence on the resulting software product in two respects. First, a relationship exists between the structure of the software team and the structure of the software system.[1] Whichever is established first will affect the structure of the other. For example, according to Weinberg, if three programmers of approximately equal ability work as a team to develop a software system, the system will probably be composed of three major components. On the other hand, if the team consists of one experienced programmer and two programmer trainees, the same application may be implemented as one major mainline component and two smaller subroutines. Because the system structure should represent a feasible, efficient solution rather than a reflection of the relationship among the team members, first the system structure should be designed and then the programming team should be organized to complement this structure.

Second, as noted in Chapter 3, the goals and priorities of the project as perceived by the team affect the software quality, and as noted in Chapter 2, team motivation affects project productivity. It is important to choose an organization that presents each individual with a clear definition of project goals, a set of challenging tasks, and a sense of purpose within the project.

In this chapter, we examine some possible organizational structures for software development teams. We are seeking an organizational structure that makes software development more visible and more amenable to management controls and state-of-the-art technologies. Such a structure should fulfill the following requirements:

1. Formalize the project so quality control standards, software engineering procedures, and management monitoring are possible
2. Promote interaction between the user, the maintainer, and the development team so that the software system will possess the qualities of usability and maintainability
3. Solve the dichotomy between the programmer's preference to work alone and the need to work as part of a team to produce a well-integrated system

We will look at three project organization concepts:

1. Egoless programming
2. Chief programmer team
3. Surgical team

Egoless programming is the least formal and the oldest of the three. The surgical team is the most specialized in its division of labor among the team members and is a refinement of the chief programmer team.

We will examine each concept to determine how well it is able to satisfy our requirements for an organizational structure. We begin with the simplest concept, egoless programming.

4.2 PROJECT TEAM ORGANIZATIONS

4.2.1 Egoless Programming

Egoless programming is the simplest team organizational structure. Its basic operating premise is that the team works toward a team goal that all member have helped to define, rather than toward separate individual goals.[2] Egoless programming stresses an open, democratic work environment (see Fig. 4.1). It removes code from the programmer's private domain by instituting code exchange as a normal part of the development process. Before compilation, each programmer requests that at least one other team member read his code and check it for errors. Also, during unit testing, each programmer consults with fellow team members as a normal part of the debugging process.

The philosophy of egoless programming is that allowing programmers to view their codes as extensions of their egos is dangerous and nonproductive. Because programmers internalize the codes they write, their coding errors are less obvious to them than to others. Encouraging a sharing of the programming process helps programmers find more errors sooner and results in code that is not only more likely to be error-free, but also more likely to be readable.

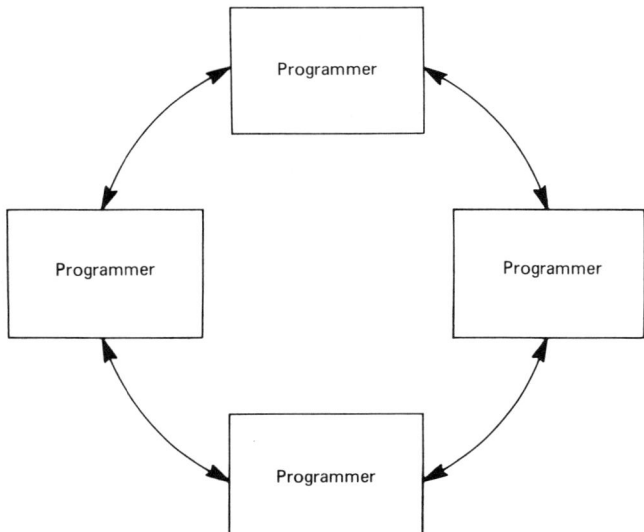

Fig. 4.1. Egoless programming organization.

This type of environment tends to reinforce the team spirit. When team members read one another's code, the total system becomes more familiar to the entire team and becomes team property, instead of an individual's private possession. The result is a better integrated system that is less dependent upon a single individual. Further, egoless programming provides an excellent learning environment. All team members, from the most experienced to the least experienced, exchange code. By sharing code, the programmers learn new programming techniques and algorithms and discuss style and efficiency questions in a nonhostile atmosphere.

Egoless programming does not suggest specific functional responsibilities for the various team members; instead, the responsibilities assigned to individual members are determined by the capabilities of members and the system structure. In this type of democratic organization, team leadership may rotate depending upon the particular skills most needed at various points in the project.

Although egoless programming provides a structure that improves system visibility, readability, and reliability, there are several problems with its democratic organization.

First, the democratic approach may be too loose a structure for imposing management controls. The functional responsibilities of each team member are not clearly defined. This is confusing to the team members, makes it difficult to evaluate the performance of an individual, and leads to motivation problems. Second, a democratic structure may be detrimental to system integrity since no one individual has the power to settle disputes arising during the project. In fact, decision-making may be postponed indefinitely as the team continues to "democratically" debate design alternatives, coding standards, test plans, and the like. Third, in times of inevitable crisis, the project may flounder as the team awaits a volunteer to take over the leadership role. Finally, team communication with outside groups such as management, the user, and other teams may be complicated since member functions are not explicitly defined and may change during the project.

4.2.2 Chief Programmer Teams

In the previous section, we found that the informal, democratic organization of egoless programming does not adequately address the areas of management control, individual responsibility, motivation and evaluation, system integrity, leadership, decision-making, and communication. In this section, we discuss a more formal team organization concept, the chief programmer team.

In contrast to the democratic structure of egoless programming, the operating premise of the chief programmer team (CPT) employs a strict organizational structure in which discipline, clear leadership, and functional separation are stressed.[3]

The goals of the CPT concept are to:

1. Structure the software development work into specific tasks for assignment to technical specialists
2. Provide an environment in which state-of-the-art tools can be readily utilized
3. Keep the software product visible throughout its development process
4. Provide a training environment for team members
5. Ensure that at least two team members understand every line of code

In the CPT, the function of each member and the relationship between members is explicitly defined. The nucleus of the team consists of two experienced technicians, called the chief programmer and the backup programmer, and a clerical assistant called the programming secretary. Additional programmers are added to the team at the discretion of the chief programmer. In some forms of the CPT, a project administrator is also included in the nucleus group. The size of a CPT ranges from seven to ten members (see Fig. 4.2).

The *chief programmer* is the undisputed technical leader of the team. In the eyes of management, he is directly responsible for the technical success of the project. His tasks include the development of the system specification and design documents, the coding and testing of the critical portions of the system, and the guidance of the other team members in the coding and testing of the remaining portions of the system. In the strictest form of the CPT, the chief programmer designs, codes, and tests every line of code in the system. In the modified form of the CPT, the chief programmer directly codes and tests only the critical portions of the system himself and supervises the coding and testing of the remaining portions of the system. The ideal

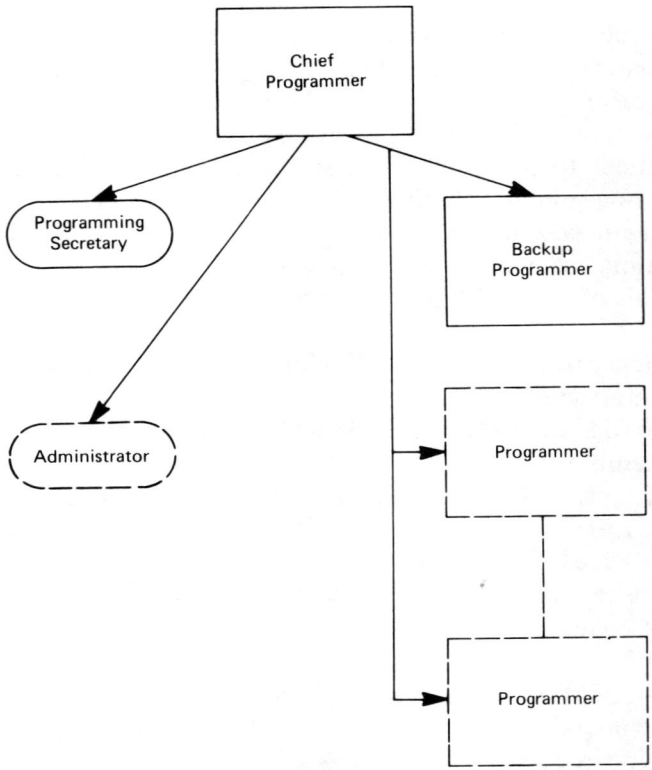

Fig. 4.2. Chief programmer team organization.

chief programmer is an expert programmer with at least ten years of software development experience.

The *backup programmer* is the backup leader of the team. Because he is totally familiar with all aspects of the project, he is prepared at any time to take over project leadership in the event that the chief programmer cannot continue. He participates in all important technical decisions, although the chief programmer has the last word in all decision-making. The tasks of the backup programmer include the development of the test plan and research activities for the chief programmer. The ideal backup programmer is also an expert programmer with several years of software development experience.

The *programming secretary* is the clerical member of the team whose principal responsibility is to keep all project documentation current and visible throughout the project. His tasks include maintenance of all program libraries, test data, test results, and project documents.

The use of standards, a development support library, and state-of-the-art software engineering tools is considered an essential component of the CPT concept.

The CPT concept formalizes the egoless programming concept in several ways. First, instead of rotating team leadership, the chief programmer assumes permanent technical leadership. With a visible leader, management controls can be more easily implemented, communication with outside groups can be simplified, and deadlock situations in decision-making can be avoided. Second, assigned tasks based upon individual characteristics are replaced by functional responsibilities clearly delineated by the specific function each member is assigned in the CPT organizational chart. With individual responsibilities defined, the contribution of each individual's efforts can be more fairly evaluated. Finally, instead of relying on code exchange to improve product visibility, a programming secretary is employed to make the most current version of the product visible to the team, to management, and to the user throughout the project. With current information readily available, a more accurate picture of project status can be reported to management and to the user.

Although we have cited several ways in which the CPT appears to provide an excellent organizational structure for meeting our requirements, there are several problems with the concept. At first glance the CPT seems to be a major step forward in an attempt to transform programming from an art to a discipline. But at second glance, it also appears to be a step backward. The CPT perpetuates the *prima donna* image of the programmer. Instead of bringing the programmer into the ganization's fold, it isolates and alienates him by encouraging the programmer to strive for a superhero image. As Hoare commented in his keynote address at the Third International Conference on Software Engineering:

> . . . there is a powerful call for a return to the age of the master craftsman—more fashionably known as a chief programmer.[4]

There are other criticisms of the CPT as well. We are seeking an organizational structure that is conducive to management control, that introduces discipline and procedures into the development process. The CPT does provide us with such a structure. But we also are seeking a structure in which programmers are motivated, challenged, and encouraged to grow professionally, a structure in which open and meaningful communication flows in and out of the project, and a structure which is practical to apply in the typical data processing organization. The CPT fails to meet these requirements.

The criticisms center around the emphasis that is placed on the chief programmer. First, we must question whether the CPT presents a challenging environment for the entire team. Certainly it is a challenging environment for the chief programmer, but what about for the other members of the team? Since the major project responsibility and the major project tasks are assigned to the chief programmer, attention is focused on the chief programmer. The tasks of the other team members seem menial in comparison. With their importance overshadowed by that of the chief programmer, the other members may lack enthusiasm. Consider, for example, the backup programmer. He is an expert with many years of experience. If he does well in this project, perhaps he may become the chief programmer in a future project. Is the role of "right hand man" challenging enough to sustain the interest of this expert throughout the project?

If we follow the strictest form of the CPT concept in which the chief programmer designs, codes, and tests every line of code, we question the quality of the learning environment provided for the other team members. Such a rigid structure is unable to build upon each individual's strengths and to improve upon each individual's weaknesses. Further, such a rigid structure may unduly influence the structure of the software being produced.

However, more serious than our concern for the morale of the team is our concern with the power given to the chief programmer. The chief programmer has the power to hire and fire every member of the team, including the administrator. He has the power to veto any team decision. He has the power to cancel the open, sharing environment encouraged by egoless programming. No checks and balances are provided to help the chief programmer curb his ego or to guard against poor technical decisions. If the software product is allowed to become the product of one rather than many minds, its quality may be jeopardized.

The chief programmer has not only too much power, but too many tasks as well. We must seriously question whether it is possible for one individual to satisfactorily execute all the functional responsibilities of the chief programmer. If it is, this is a rare individual, unlikely to be found in the typical data processing organization. This brings us to the question of feasibility. There simply are not enough qualified chief programmers available to make the CPT a practical concept in the data processing organization.

4.2.3 Surgical Team

In the surgical team, the functional responsibilities of each member of the CPT are further delineated.[5] The surgical team is composed of a group of highly specialized technicians supported by an administrator, an editor, and clerical assistants (see Fig. 4.3). Each team member is given a title describing his primary function—surgeon, copilot, administrator, editor, secretary, program clerk, toolsmith, tester, and language lawyer.

The *surgeon* is the technical manager of the team and performs the same function as the chief programmer. The surgeon's tasks include defining the functional specifications and the design; writing and testing the code; and producing the technical documentation.

The *copilot* performs the same functions as the backup programmer and, in addition, provides an interface with other teams.

Although included in only some versions of the chief programmer team, the *administrator* is a core member of the surgical team, responsible for handling project personnel, budgeting matters, procurement of space, computer time and technical tools and provides an interface with management. The administrator reports to the surgeon and must obtain the surgeon's approval in making administrative decisions.

The clerical staff consists of an editor, two secretaries, and a program clerk. Using the documentation draft of the surgeon, the *editor* generates all project documentation including internal system documentation, user manuals, and operations manuals. One secretary performs clerical functions for the editor and the other secretary performs clerical functions for the administrator and the team. The *program clerk* performs the same function as the programming secretary of the CPT.

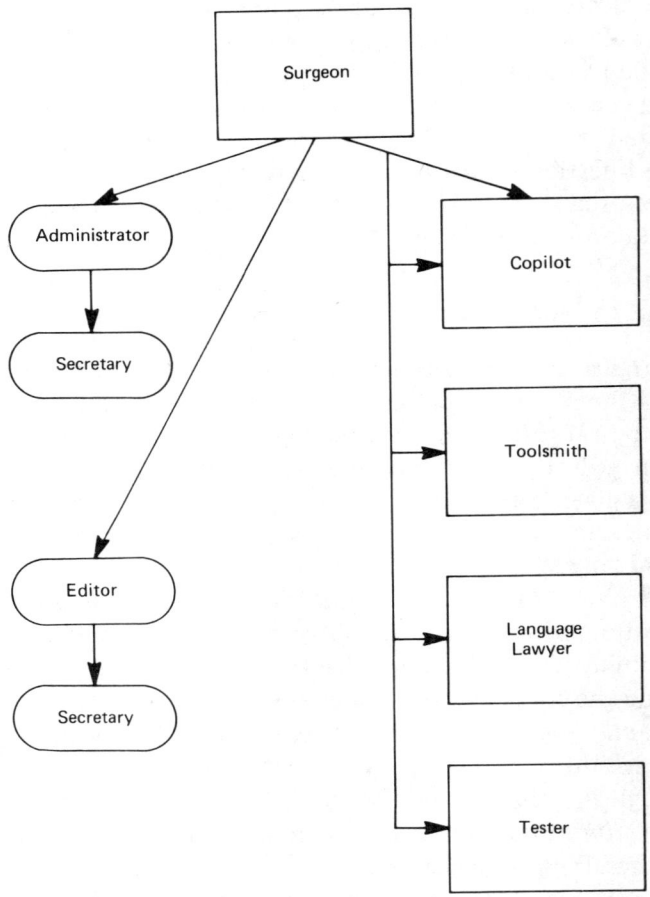

Fig. 4.3. Surgical team organization.

The surgical team refines the functions of the programmers in the CPT by defining the toolsmith, tester, and language lawyer specialists. The *toolsmith* is responsible for providing to the team all necessary technical tools. His tasks include construction of specialized utilities, catalogued procedures, and macro libraries, and the support of editors, interactive debuggers, preprocessors, and so forth. The *tester* implements the test plan that was defined by the surgeon, by creating test data, test driver programs, and debugging procedures. The *language lawyer* serves as resident expert on the programming languages used by the team and researches the most efficient ways to implement the design specifications as well-structured code.

The surgical team responds to some of the criticisms of the CPT by addressing:

- the issues of team morale and individual recognition
- the importance of a communication link and quality documentation

Although the surgeon is the technical manager and retains total technical responsibility for the project, the other team members are recognized as experts in their own right. The copilot expands the status and visibility of the backup programmer by providing the very important communication function with other teams. Each programmer improves his visibility by specializing in a particular technical skill. An editor is included in the team to produce professional documentation for the system.

As with the CPT, the major criticism of the surgical team lies with the surgeon. The surgeon, just as the chief programmer, has too many functions to perform and too much power. Also, just as for the chief programmer, the surgeon's technical skills are emphasized over management and leadership skills. The project case histories presented in Chapter 2 demonstrated the importance of good project management in ensuring project success. The project leader should be trained in project management skills as well as in technical skills, and should function more as a leader and less as a "doer." In the next section, we propose a revised CPT concept in which the project leader is viewed as a leader rather than a "super-programmer."

4.3 REVISED CHIEF PROGRAMMER TEAM

4.3.1 Project Organization Requirements

Before we present our definition of the revised chief programmer team, let us review our requirements for a project organization structure. We are seeking a structure that accomplishes the following:

1. Enhances software product visibility so that the software can be subjected to periodic audit reviews during development

2. Formalizes the project organization so that individual responsibilities and assignments are clearly defined
3. Establishes communication links between the project and the outside organization including management, the user, other teams, and the operations and maintenance groups
4. Encourages an open, egoless environment in which state-of-the-art tools can be mastered and applied
5. Avoids project dependency upon individual team members

The structure we propose to satisfy these requirements is based upon the CPT concept. It combines the discipline of the CPT and the specialization of function of the surgical team and reintroduces the sharing of egoless programming. We refer to this structure as the *Revised Chief Programmer Team* (RCPT).

4.3.2 RCPT Structure

The nucleus of the RCPT consists of a project leader, a project co-leader, a user liaison, and a project administrator (see Fig. 4.4). The team can be expanded to include a technical writer and a team of programmers. As we look at Fig. 4.4, we can immediately see one difference between the CPT and the RCPT. In the RCPT, the project leader, who is the counterpart of the chief programmer, reports to the administrator rather than vice versa. This is one method for limiting the scope of responsibilities for the project leader. We will discuss this in more detail later in this section. Next, we define the function of each member in the RCPT (see Fig. 4.5).

The *project leader* is the technical leader of the team, responsible for software product development. He reports to the project administrator, and all other team members report to him. He is active in the project from its inception through turnover. As his title suggests, his primary function is as technical director, not as chief coder. The tasks of the project leader include:

1. Determining project resource requirements with the project administrator
2. Developing and enforcing standards and procedures
3. Producing functional specifications and design documents with the assistance of the co-leader and the user liaison

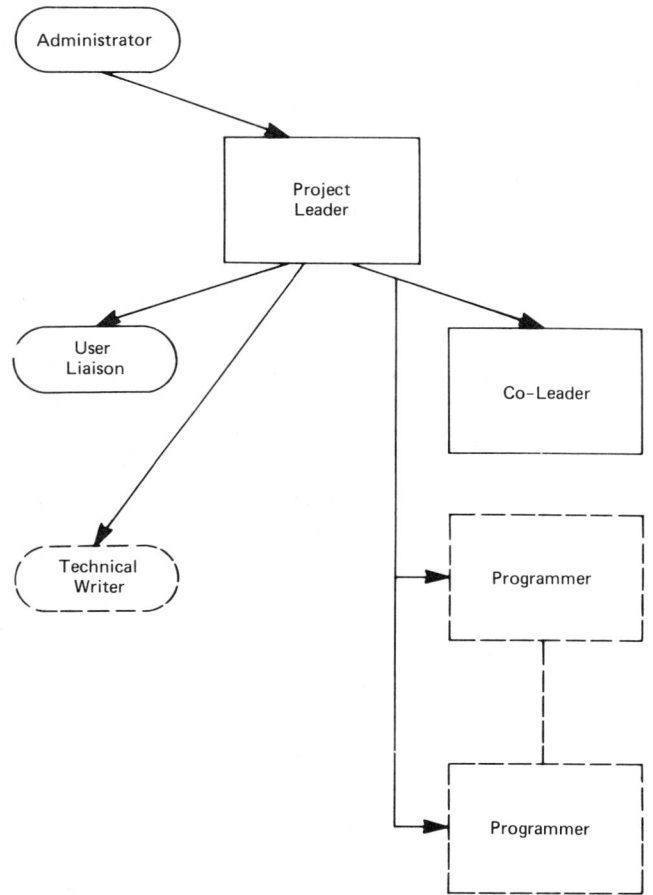

Fig. 4.4. Revised chief programmer team organization.

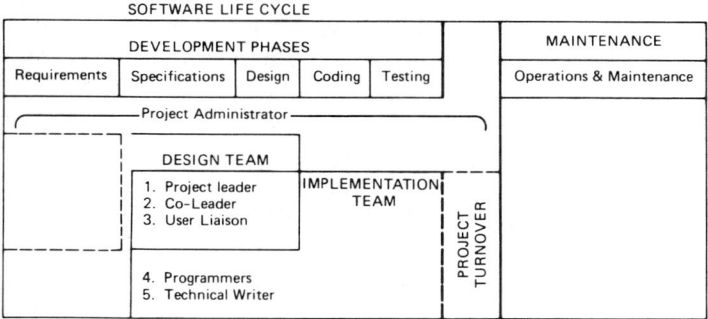

Fig. 4.5. RCPT participation in the software life cycle.

4. Assigning and managing all technical tasks
5. Reviewing all code
6. Reviewing the test plan and test results
7. Writing internal system documentation
8. Keeping a project journal
9. Increasing the expertise of each team member

The *co-leader* performs a function similar to that of the CPT backup programmer. As his title suggests, he is the technical assistant of the project leader. He is groomed by the project leader to assume the team leadership role in the event that the project leader cannot complete the project, and is active in the project from its inception through turnover. His responsibilities are expanded from those of the backup programmer in that he serves as the co-designer with the project leader and the user liaison during the specifications and design phases. However, the project leader retains the final say on all technical decisions. Like the project leader, the co-leader is an experienced analyst, rather than a "super-programmer." His tasks include:

1. Co-producing the system specifications and design documents with the project leader and the user liaison
2. Developing a project test plan
3. Reviewing code and test results with the project leader
4. Investigating development problems
5. Representing the team in technical meetings with outside groups
6. Coordinating project turnover with maintenance group

The *project administrator* is the administrative head of the team. As project manager, he performs the interface function with upper management. He provides the team with necessary resources, protects the team from outside interference, and handles its public relations and visibility to the outside organization. He is active in the project from inception through turnover. His tasks include:

1. Explaining to the team the project objectives and priorities as defined by management
2. Providing a suitable work environment and necessary resources for the team

3. Handling the project budget
4. Handling the recruiting and performance evaluation of team personnel
5. Reporting project status and needs to upper management and the user

The *user liaison* provides the communication link between the team and the user. Most probably, he comes from the user community, rather than from the technical area. Although he may have programming skills, the emphasis is placed on his knowledge of the application area and his ability to translate user needs, priorities and requirements into technical terms. He is active in the project from its inception through turnover. His tasks include:

1. Responsibility for the software product meeting user requirements and expectations
2. Interpretation of user requirements to technical members of the team
3. Production of user documentation
4. Handling of public relations of the project team with the user community
5. Participation in testing, particularly in the construction of system and acceptance test cases and test data
6. Coordinating project turnover with the team, the user, and the operations and maintenance groups

The *programmers* are responsible for performing the coding and the testing functions of the project. They use the functional specifications and design documents to produce an efficient, well-structured software system fulfilling user requirements. Tasks are assigned to the programmers by the project leader on the basis of their individual skills and experience. As in the surgical team, the programmers may specialize in certain functions such as coding or testing. However, the RCPT permits more of the egoless programming informality of rotating functions at the programmer level since the team is likely to be composed of a mix of experienced and trainee level programmers. The programmers participate in the project from the program design through the testing phases. Their tasks include:

1. Responsibility for coding
2. Construction of specialized utilities, catalogued procedures, macro libraries, etc
3. Adaptation of packages and existing routines for incorporation into the system
4. Responsibility for developing unit test plans and performing testing.

4.3.3 Comparison of RCPT and CPT

Our primary motivation for modifying the CPT is our concern with the chief programmer function. Our intention is to limit the tasks and limit the power of the chief programmer (surgeon). In the RCPT, we attempt not only to spread the work but also to spread a sense of recognition and a sense of purpose among all team members. This is accomplished by redistributing some of the chief programmer responsibilities to the co-leader, the administrator, and the programmers. The chief programmer function is refined to emphasize conceptual and leadership abilities over programming skills.

In comparing the chief programmer and the project leader, we see several differences. First, whereas the chief programmer is an expert programmer, the project leader is an expert conceptualizer, designer, and project manager, but not necessarily a "super-programmer." Because he possesses both project management and technical skills and because his programming tasks have been reassigned to other team members, he is able to direct, oversee, and review all technical functions in the project. For example, the project manager does no actual coding, but he does read every line of code to ensure that it meets specifications and standards requirements.

Second, some of the power of the chief programmer has been reassigned to the project administrator. Because the administrator is a member of management, he understands the budget, the market, and the total organization. The higher his management level, the better. He can use his weight to gather the resources and support needed for the project and to gain recognition for the team. He also can use his power to provide a check and balance system for the project leader. For example, the administrator is responsible for recruiting and evaluating project personnel. Of course, he should consult the project leader when making these decisions. One administrator should be able to perform the administrative functions for several RCPTs.

Third, since he is relieved from responsibilities requiring his interaction with upper management and other outside groups, the project leader can focus his attention on managing the team. As project manager, he is responsible for the well-being and professional growth of each team member. He can divide his time among the programmers according to their assignments and their need for supervision. Carefully preserving the delicate balance between what is good for the individual and what is good for the team, he can develop a program for each team member to accommodate special strengths and weaknesses.

A second motivation for modifying the CPT is to improve the project communication with the outside organization. As mentioned earlier in this chapter, this is important for several reasons. Past projects have shown that we are unlikely to make programmers cognizant of their role in the organization or to dispel the mystery of computers as long as programmers are permitted to work in isolation. The RCPT establishes explicit communication links with various groups outside the team to improve project visibility and product quality (see Fig. 4.6).

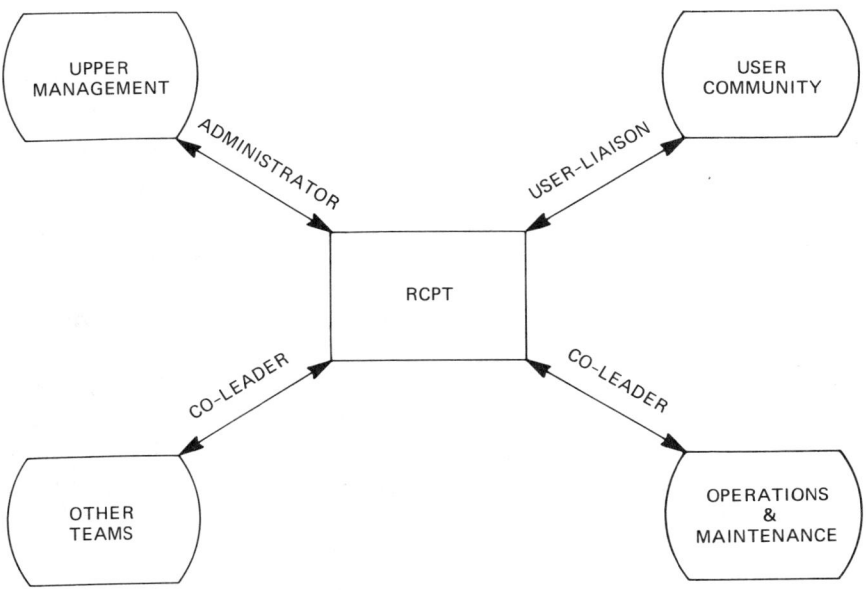

Fig. 4.6. RCPT communication links.

From the viewpoint of the system maintainer, communication with the development team is imperative. As discussed in Chapter 3, the maintainer should participate in every phase of software development to ensure the software qualities of usability, reliability, and maintainability. He must become familiar with the system to prepare for its support in an operations environment and to evaluate its impact on existing systems. As he learns about the proposed system, he can suggest existing modules, programs, and packages to be used in the development of this system, and he can react to the design implementation feasibility. As an interested third party, he can review the completeness of the test plan and can participate in the testing process. The project co-leader serves as the maintainer's link to the development activities. The co-leader provides the maintainer with the system requirements, specifications, design, test plans and development schedule, invites the maintainer to project review sessions, and defines the maintainer's role in the testing process.

A communication link between the user and the team is established by the user liaison. Although considered a technical success, many projects have failed because the software did not satisfy user requirements. The need to communicate effectively and continually with the user during software development cannot be overemphasized. It is the liaison's responsibility to ensure the software quality of usability from the user's viewpoint. The user group can be informed of system progress and assured that its voice is heard and understood throughout the project via the liaison. Also, because many software systems suffer from poor user documenention, the user liaison concentrates on the publication of timely and understandable documentation.

Project visibility to management is the responsibility of the project administrator who speaks the same language as management and is therefore able to provide management with meaningful project information.

We conclude our comparison of the CPT and the RCPT by examining the ease with which these two concepts can be applied in a typical data processing organization. We consider the RCPT the more practical of the two because it does not rely on the "super-ability" of a chief programmer. Instead, it is headed by a project leader who has

ORGANIZING THE SOFTWARE DEVELOPMENT TEAM 89

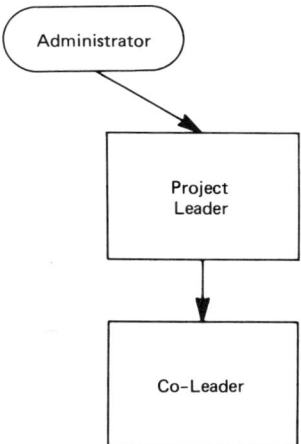

Fig. 4.7. Contracted RCPT organization.

solid technical skills plus project management experience. The skills of the project leader are more likely to be found, and more likely to be useful, in a data processing organization than those of the chief programmer. Although the RCPT depends upon discipline, standards, and procedures, it also concentrates on the human aspects of the team. The project leader is responsible for the professional growth of the team as well as for the development of a software product. If the case histories of the IFMS-I Report Generator and the SMCS Charting projects discussed in Chapter 2 do not simply represent some isolated incidents, we see that human factors can greatly influence project success.

Because it is a more flexible structure than the CPT, the RCPT can be contracted to accommodate small projects or expanded to accommodate large projects. For small projects, the RCPT can be contracted to include only the project leader and the co-leader (see Fig. 4.7). The project leader and the co-leader can jointly perform the user liaison and the programmer functions in addition to performing their individual functions. One administrator can handle more than one small project. For large projects, a hierarchy of RCPTs can be formed, with the co-leader acting as the link between teams, and with one overall project administrator (see Fig. 4.8).

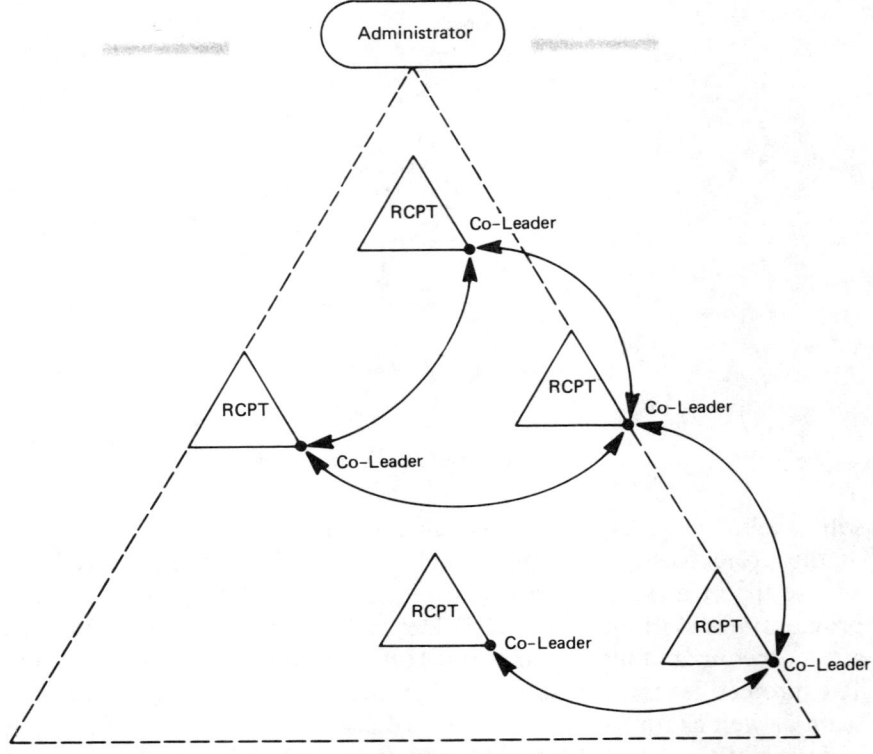

Fig. 4.8. Hierarchy of RCPTs.

4.4 SUMMARY

In this chapter, we discussed three software project organization concepts:

1. Egoless programming
2. Chief programmer team
3. Surgical team

We evaluated each concept in terms of its ability to:

1. Enhance software product visibility
2. Introduce functional formality into the team tasks

ORGANIZING THE SOFTWARE DEVELOPMENT TEAM

3. Establish communication links with the outside organization
4. Encourage an open, egoless atmosphere
5. Avoid project dependency on one individual

Because we found major shortcomings with each of the above three concepts, we created a fourth organization concept, the Revised chief programmer team (RCPT). It combines the discipline of the chief programmer team, the specialization of function in the surgical team, and the democracy of egoless programming. The RCPT emphasizes the need for a project leader with project management skills and the need for communication mechanisms with the outside organization. The nucleus group in the RCPT consists of a project leader, a co-leader, an administrator and a user liaison. The RCPT is a practical concept that can be applied in a typical data processing organization since it does not rely on "super-programmers."

We shall look at the RCPT concept again when we discuss the organization of the maintenance staff in Part III.

5
Controlling Software Development

5.1 INTRODUCTION

Because so much attention has been given to the individual project phases of software development, but relatively little to coordinating the whole process, control problems often arise. The project coordination task is very complex and continually demands management decisions. In fact, the coordinating/control effort is more difficult than performing any individual project phase. When management control procedures are not used, problems can persist unrecognized and unsolved, ultimately causing project failure.

We turn to the project case studies presented in Chapter 2 to illustrate this danger. Recall that a primary reason for the failure of the GIRG project was poor project management. Because the GIRG project was a small and familiar application, formal project management controls were not used. There was no formal organization, no clear definition of individual responsibilities and assignments, and no formal status reporting structure. This lack of formal structure made it impossible for management to control and monitor the GIRG project. On the other hand, a primary reason for the success of the SMCS Charting project was the systematic, disciplined software development approach used. Individual team responsibilities and project tasks were carefully defined making project management control and monitoring possible.

In this chapter we focus our attention on the control aspects of project management. We cannot overemphasize the importance of providing adequate management controls in software projects. Control is necessary for project visibility, for a system of checks and balances, and for meaningful communication with the user and the maintainer. Through control mechanisms, management can introduce discipline and procedures into a project and measure their utility, can recognize and reward individual accomplishments, and can become aware of problems and take steps to remedy them as soon as they arise.

Our project management philosophy is that management control should be planned, consistent, and knowledgeable of the project implications of each management decision.[1] Above all, it should not be reactionary, of the "fire-fighting" sort that is so typical of many projects. The attitude that "this time we will just do it and next time we will use sound project management and software engineering principles" must stop, because the result of this attitude is software that does not serve the user. Except in rare cases, there is no time to redo software because the backlog of requested applications is growing at a rate far, far greater than our ability to develop new software.

Germane to our approach for project control are:

1. Identification of project responsibilities
2. Introduction of formal control mechanisms
3. Inclusion of acceptance criteria and acceptance procedures
4. Inclusion of problem resolution procedures and change procedures

This approach provides integrated and formal management controls that continually evaluate project progress to give management current and realistic information for making decisions that are better suited for the good of the whole project, rather than just the concerns of the current development phase. We discuss this approach in detail in the sections that follow.

5.2 PROJECT RESPONSIBILITIES

At project inception, project team responsibilities must be clearly defined along with project objectives and priorities. Each team member should be made aware of who is responsible for what and what is the chain of command. Without a clearly defined authority structure, project control becomes an impossibility, project decision-making may be impaired, system integrity may be threatened, and accurate status information may be unavailable.

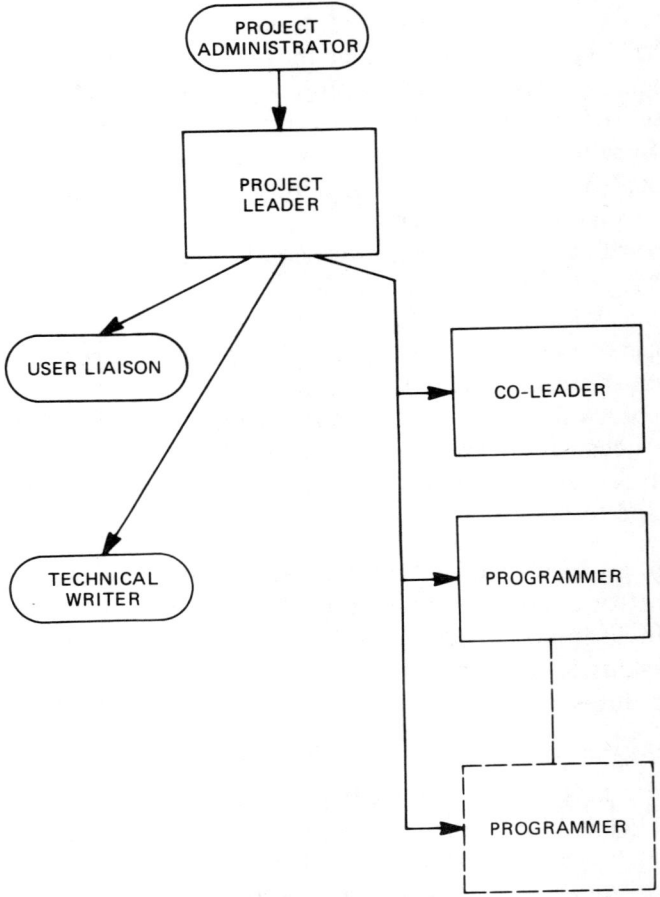

Fig. 5.1. Revised chief programmer team.

The Revised Chief Programmer Team structure (RCPT) presented in Chapter 4 can be used to identify the basic project authority/responsibility structure (see Fig. 5.1). In the RCPT structure, the project administrator bears the overall responsibility for the project, i.e., for producing a quality software product meeting user requirements and expectations within schedule and cost estimates. The project leader is directly responsible for the technical production of the software. In the RCPT structure, management knows to whom to direct project status questions, general information questions, requests, and concerns.

Table 5.1. SMCS Project Management Assignments.

RESPONSIBILITY	SYSTEM DEVELOPMENT PHASES				
	REQUIREMENTS	SPECIFICATIONS	DESIGN	CODE	TEST
Project Leader (overall project responsibility)	▲	▲	▲	▲	▲
Design Manager (performed by project leader)		▲	▲		
Implementation Manager (performed by Chief programmer)				▲	▲

In many projects, it is useful to further delegate project responsibilities. For example, when project development phases must overlap in the interest of compressing many man-years of effort into a few development years, separate project groups are organized to work on particular project phases in parallel. Recall the SMCS Charting Project from Chapter 2 (see Chapter 2, Fig. 2.1). The SMCS project team was divided into two work groups, the design group and the implementation group. The design group was responsible for the specification and design phases; the implementation group was responsible for the coding and testing phases (see Table 5.1). When the design of a major portion of the SMCS system was completed, its implementation was begun while the design work for the remaining portions of the SMCS system continued. This approach works well only when the responsibilities of each group are clearly defined and a communication channel for conveying project information, relating to both status and software product, exists between the project groups and management. For example, the SMCS implementation group received from the design group the current and correct version of the specifications, the design, and the test plan. The design group, on the other hand, was informed of specification errors, design problems, and implementation infeasibilites discovered by the implementation group.

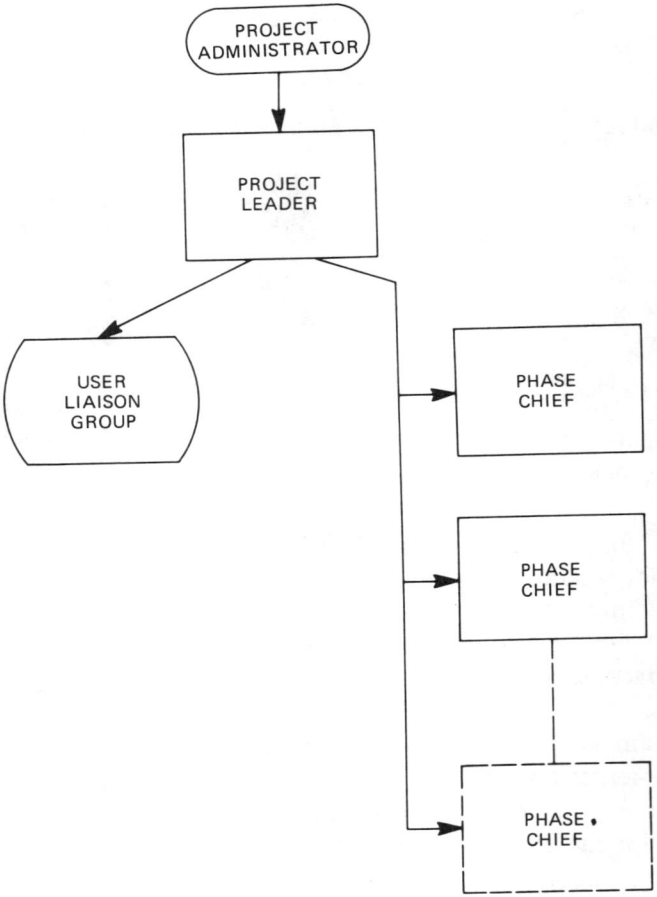

Fig. 5.2. Project phase group organization.

In large projects, it may be necessary to form a separate project group devoted to each development phase (see Fig. 5.2). Each group is managed by a *phase chief* who is directly responsible for the execution of all the phase tasks on schedule within cost estimates and for the production of correct, quality software deliverables complying with company defined standards and procedures. Note that each phase chief reports to the project leader. The organizational structure of each phase group is based upon the RCPT structure. For example, the design group may consist of a group of analysts organized as shown

CONTROLLING SOFTWARE DEVELOPMENT 97

in Fig. 5.3. The design phase chief may provide the communication function to outside groups himself or delegate this responsibility to one of the group analysts.

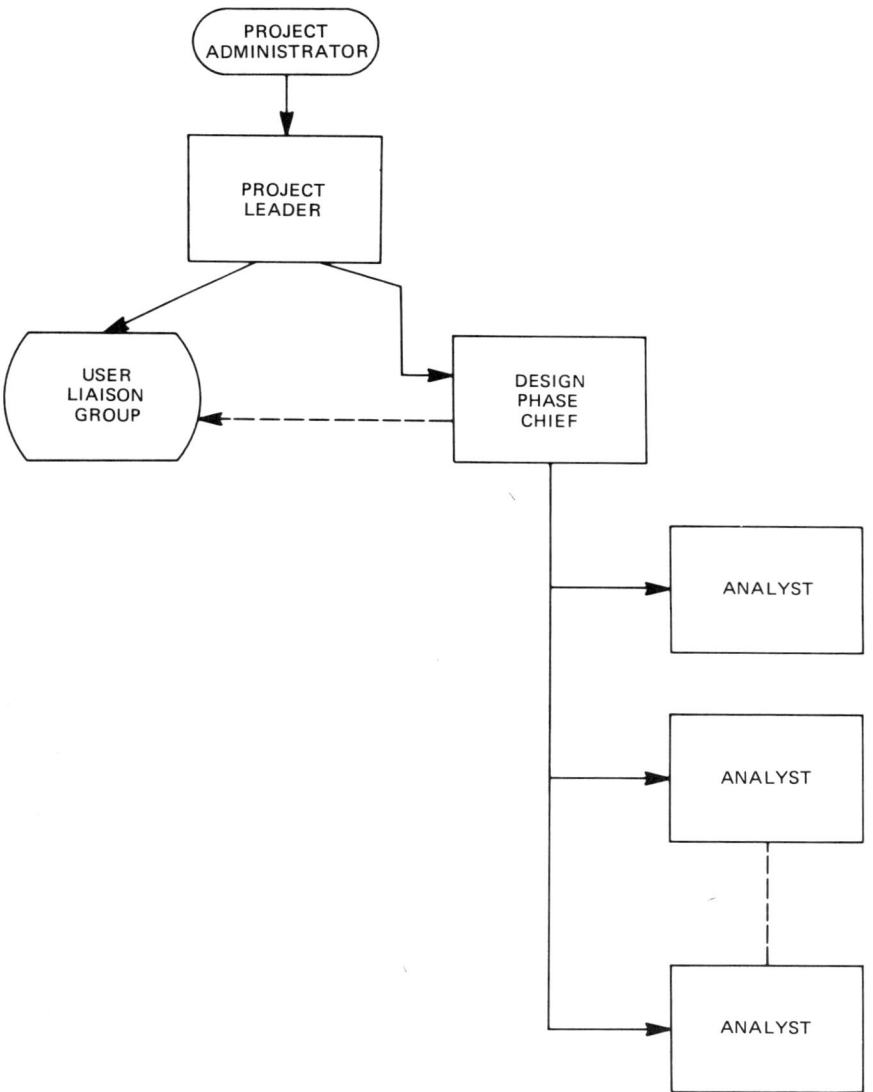

Fig. 5.3. Design phase group.

98 PART 2 MANAGING SOFTWARE DEVELOPMENT

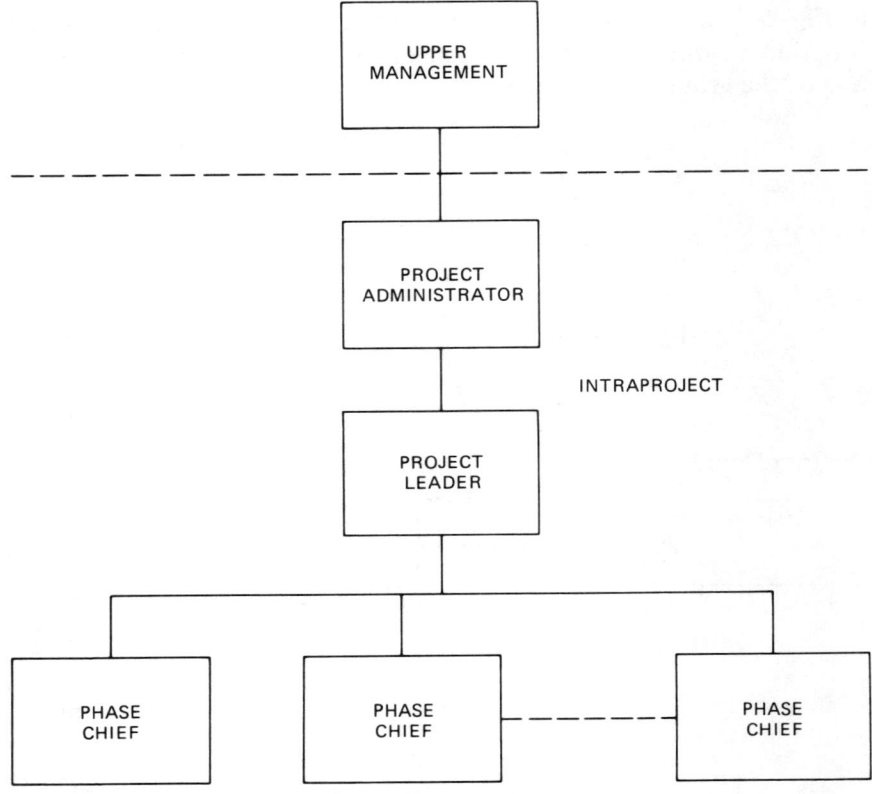

Fig. 5.4. Project management levels.

This extended project structure creates four basic management levels (see Fig. 5.4).

1. Upper management
2. Project Administrator
3. Project Leader
4. Phase Chief

To keep each management level informed of current project status and problems, the reporting structure is formalized and control documents are required. We discuss this further in the next two sections.

5.3 PROJECT CONTROL MECHANISMS

5.3.1 Introduction

Project control is the management function of evaluating and regulating project activities to assure the achievement of project objectives.[2] As we discussed earlier in this chapter, project control requires a clear definition of project goals, priorities, and responsibilities. It also requires mechanisms for obtaining and recording accurate status information and mechanisms for evaluating project progress and product qualities in terms of company standards and procedures.

In this chapter, we discuss four basic mechanisms for project control:

1. Reviews
2. Status reporting
3. Control documents
4. System development journal

Each of these mechanisms serves to improve for management the visibility and understandability of the technical activities that make up a software project.

5.3.2 Project Reviews

5.3.2.1 Structured Walk-Through. We suggest two kinds of project reviews:

1. Check-point reviews
2. Introduction reviews

Check-point reviews are used to ensure adherence to standards and procedures, to ensure quality control, to supply project status information, and to provide software product deliverables including documentation to the appropriate recipient groups. They occur at project milestones, scheduled at the completion of each development phase. Introduction reviews are used to introduce a project phase to the project team, to assign individual responsibilities and tasks, and to review the input to that project phase. All reviews are conducted following a structured walk-through format.

A *structured walk-through* is a formalized review process consisting of a set of rules for reviewing software development progress. It is used to:

- Determine schedule breakdowns
- Introduce a software development task to a project team or phase group
- Identify problems, oversights, inconsistencies, and errors
- Provide a constructive environment in which to learn and exchange ideas

The basic rules for a structured walk-through are:[3]

1. A walk-through is *not* used as a means to review an individual's work performance; it *is* used as a means to review software as it is being developed.
2. Each person attending a walk-through must function in one of the following roles:
    - Reviewee
    - Reviewer
    - Recording Secretary (usually one of the reviewers).
3. The reviewee conducts the meeting, since it is this person's material that will be reviewed.
4. The reviewee is responsible for distributing the material to be reviewed (or an outline of the material, at the very least) to the reviewers, and for allowing them adequate time to look it over before the walk-through (usually two working days).
5. The reviewee is responsible for arranging the time and place of the walk-through and for notifying the reviewers.
6. Normally, the walk-through should not exceed two hours. It should begin promptly at the indicated starting time.

CONTROLLING SOFTWARE DEVELOPMENT 101

7. The optimal number of persons attending a walk-through is four to six.
8. The purpose of the walk-through is to familiarize the reviewers with the material and to identify actual or potential problems. Problems may be assigned but are *not* corrected during the walk-through.
9. All problems identified and assignments made during the walk-through are recorded by the recording secretary.

There are five basic steps to be followed in a structured walk-through:

1. Each reviewer is asked by the reviewee to point out possible problems discovered when the material was initially reviewed before the walk-through. Problems should be recorded on an Incident Report form (see Table 5.2).
2. The reviewee gives an overview of the material.
3. The reviewee "walks through" the material in a step-by-step fashion noting problems mentioned by the reviewers.
4. Assignments are made to specific individuals to investigate and correct problems identified during the walk-through.
5. A Phase Acceptance form (see Tables 5.3–5.7) or Introduction Review form (see Table 5.10) is filled out by the reviewee and signed by each reviewer with a copy placed in the System Development Journal.

5.3.2.2 Check-points and Freeze-points. We use the five software development phases to mark project check-points at which management can assess project progress in terms of:

- Schedule
- Quality control
- Coordination
- User satisfaction

Table 5.2. Incident Report.

Table 5.2
Incident Report

APPLICATION: _____ REPORTER: _____
PROGRAM: _____ DATE: _____
SUB/MOD: _____

DESCRIPTION OF INCIDENT:

POTENTIAL PROBLEMS:

RECOMMENDED ACTION:

Table 5.3. Requirements Phase Acceptance.

Table 5.3
Requirements Phase Acceptance

APPLICATION: _____ PROGRAM: _____

DELIVERABLES CHECKLIST

_____ Project Objectives and Priorities

_____ Project Schedule

_____ System Resources and Constraints

_____ System Requirements

ASSIGNMENTS:
_____
_____
_____
_____
_____

REVIEWEE: _____ DATE: _____

REVIEWERS   DATE
_____   _____
_____   _____
_____   _____
_____   _____
_____   _____

104 PART 2 MANAGING SOFTWARE DEVELOPMENT

Table 5.4. Specification Phase Acceptance.

Table 5.4
Specification Phase Acceptance

APPLICATION: _____ PROGRAM _____

DELIVERABLES CHECKLIST

_____ System Objectives   _____ Development Schedule

_____ System Specifications   _____ Project Control Plan

_____ System Structure Chart   _____ Impact Statements

_____ Data Flow Diagram   _____ Test Plan

_____ Data I/O Descriptions   _____ Cost/Benefit Analysis

_____ Table Descriptions   _____ Recommendation

_____ File Access   _____ System Development Journal

_____ Data Bases   _____ Training

ASSIGNMENTS:
_____
_____
_____
_____
_____

REVIEWEE: _____   DATE: _____

REVIEWERS   DATE

Table 5.5. Design Phase Acceptance.

```
                        Table 5.5
                  Design Phase Acceptance


    APPLICATION: _____ PROGRAM: _____
    SUBROUTINE/MODULE: _____


    DELIVERABLES CHECKLIST

    _____ Objective/Function          _____ Data Structures

    _____ Specifications              _____ Data Bases

    _____ Descriptive Narrative/Algorithm _____ Edits

    _____ Support Documentation       _____ Contingency Plans

    _____ Structure Chart/HIPO Diagrams _____ Future Changes

    _____ Data Flow Diagram           _____ System Development
                                                      Journal
    _____ Table Descriptions

    _____ Files


    ASSIGNMENTS:
    _____
    _____
    _____
    _____
    _____


    REVIEWEE: _____       DATE: _____


    REVIEWERS                             DATE
    _____         _____
    _____         _____
    _____         _____
    _____         _____
```

Table 5.6. Coding Phase Acceptance.

Table 5.6
Coding Phase Acceptance

APPLICATION: _____ PROGRAM: _____
SUBROUTINE/MODULE: _____

DELIVERABLES CHECKLIST FOR PROGRAM SUPPORT

_____ Program Listings   _____ Unit Test History

_____ Program Libraries   _____ Complexity Profile

_____ Job Control   _____ System Development Journal

DELIVERABLES CHECKLIST FOR OPERATIONS SUPPORT

_____ Computing Requirements

_____ General Operations Information

_____ Job Control

_____ Maintainability Plan

ASSIGNMENTS
_____
_____
_____
_____

REVIEWERS   DATE
_____   _____
_____   _____
_____   _____
_____   _____
_____   _____

REVIEWEE: _____   DATE: _____

Table 5.7. Testing Phase Acceptance.

Table 5.7
Testing Phase Acceptance

APPLICATION: _____ PROGRAM: _____
SUBROUTINE/MODULE _____

TEST DELIVERABLES CHECKLIST

_____ Program Listings
_____ Program Libraries
_____ Test History
_____ Error Statistics
_____ System Development Journal

ASSIGNMENTS
_____
_____
_____
_____
_____

REVIEWEE: _____ DATE: _____

REVIEWERS   DATE
_____   _____
_____   _____
_____   _____
_____   _____
_____   _____

Check-points (also called milestones) occur at the end of each development phase (see Fig. 5.5) and are formalized as a structured review to demonstrate that specific procedures have been performed and that specific software deliverables and documentation have been produced and are available for subsequent project activities. They are a means of incorporating explicit audit steps into the development process to assess software quality. During a check-point review, the software is audited for compliance to standards and to quality control criteria. For example, the maintainer evaluates the software in terms of its ability to meet minimal maintainability requirements such as documentation, structuring, complexity, and testing. Identifying quality deficiencies during the development process will greatly improve the chances of producing quality controlled software.

Formality is required in check-point reviews due to the complexity of software projects, the abstract nature of software products, and the number of people involved. Without formality, the management view of progress is in terms of percent complete figures that rarely report anything about true project status and problems. This is why management has so often been surprised to learn that a two-year project reported to be 95 percent complete for the last six months will now be a year late.

The check-point review is conducted by the person responsible for that project phase using the format of a structured walk-through. It is attended by each project phase chief (or his phase co-leader), the project leader and/or co-leader, the user liaison, the maintainer, and the quality control group responsible for enforcing company standards and software quality.

During the check-point review the following activities occur:

- Software product deliverables and documents produced by this project phase are turned over.
- Problems that may affect other project phases are identified.
- Project schedule status is discussed.
- Change requests are discussed.

The material to be reviewed includes the software deliverables produced during the project phase and any unresolved Incident Reports

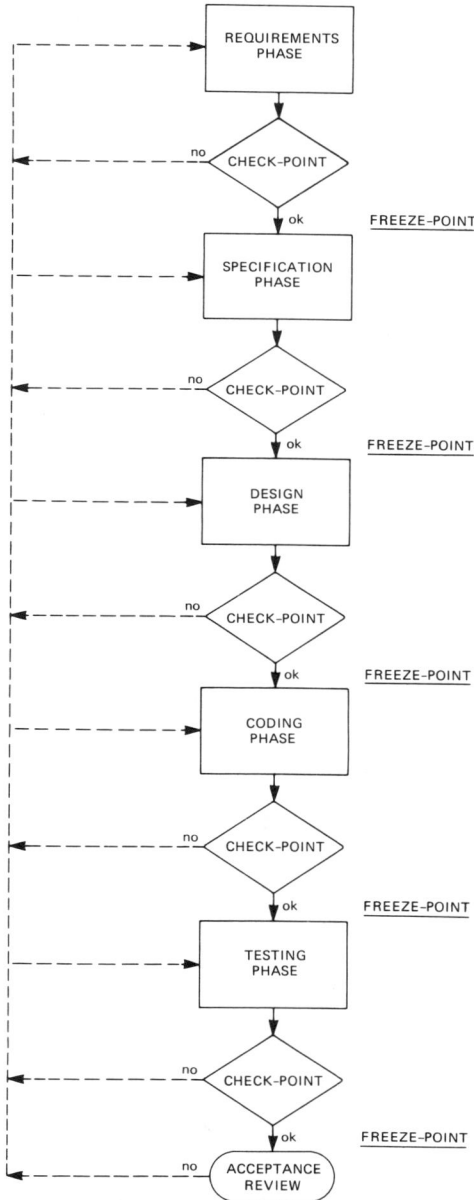

Fig. 5.5. Software development check-points.

110 PART 2 MANAGING SOFTWARE DEVELOPMENT

generated by that phase. A list of the minimal set of deliverables to be produced by each phase and to be used as input to successive phases is shown in Fig. 5.6–Fig. 5.9.

Each problem arising during the phase should be documented on an Incident Report form (see Table 5.2). Unresolved problems should

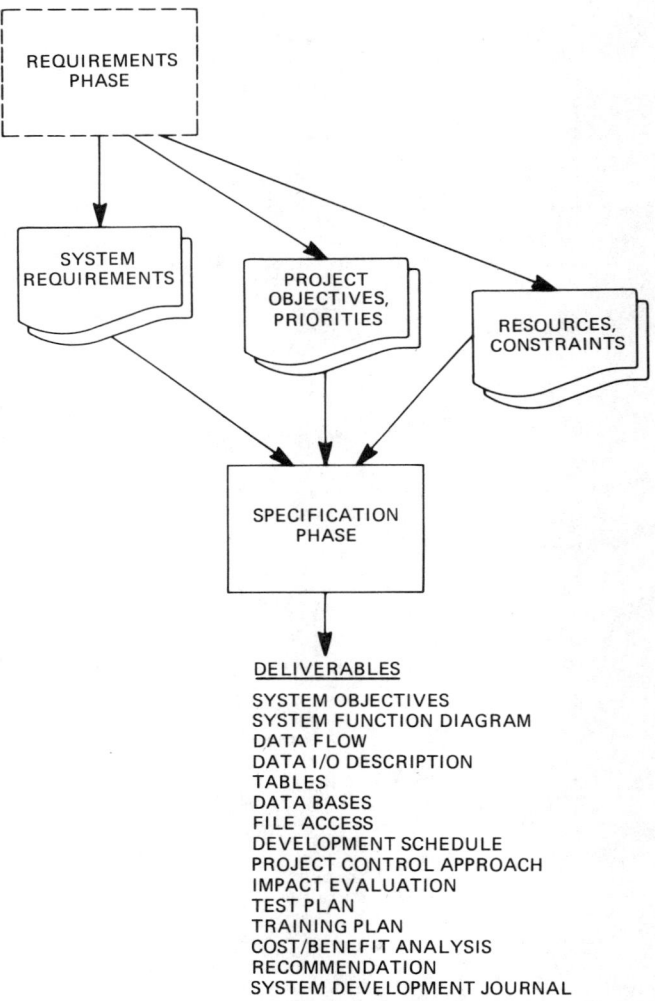

Fig. 5.6. Specification phase deliverables.

be identified during the check-point review. Followup action to investigate and to resolve these problems should be assigned to specific individuals and noted in the Phase Acceptance document (see Tables 5.3–5.7). It is the responsibility of the reviewee to make certain that there is a followup of each problem identified during the check-point

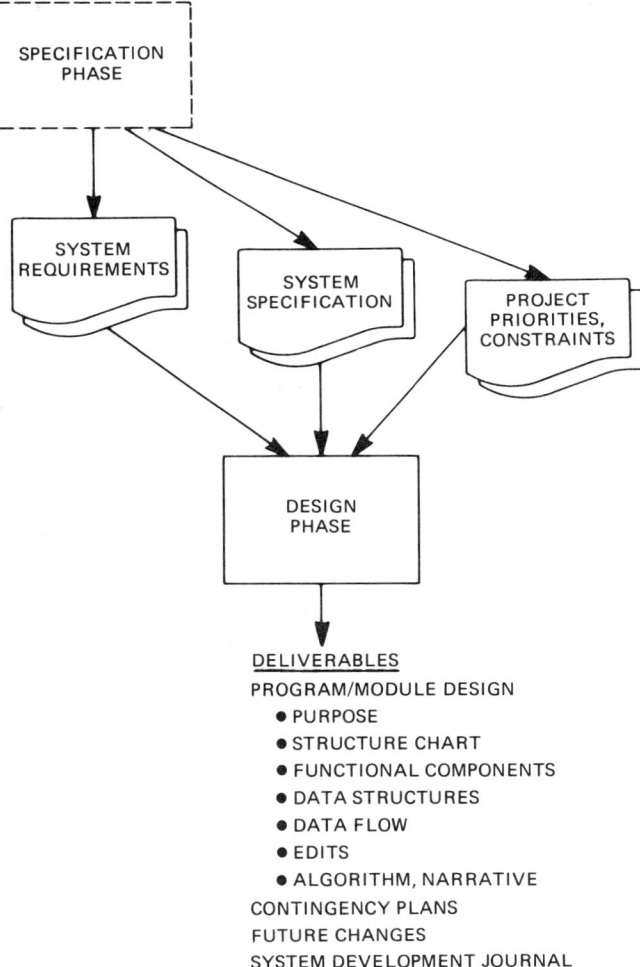

Fig. 5.7. Design phase deliverables.

112   PART 2   MANAGING SOFTWARE DEVELOPMENT

walk-through. The Phase Acceptance document is signed by each person attending the check-point review to signify his approval of the completeness of the review and the quality of the material reviewed (with the exceptions noted). It is possible for the review group to recommend that the project not proceed until certain noted deficiencies are corrected. The signed Phase Acceptance document becomes a permanent project control document. We discuss control documents further in Section 5.3.4.

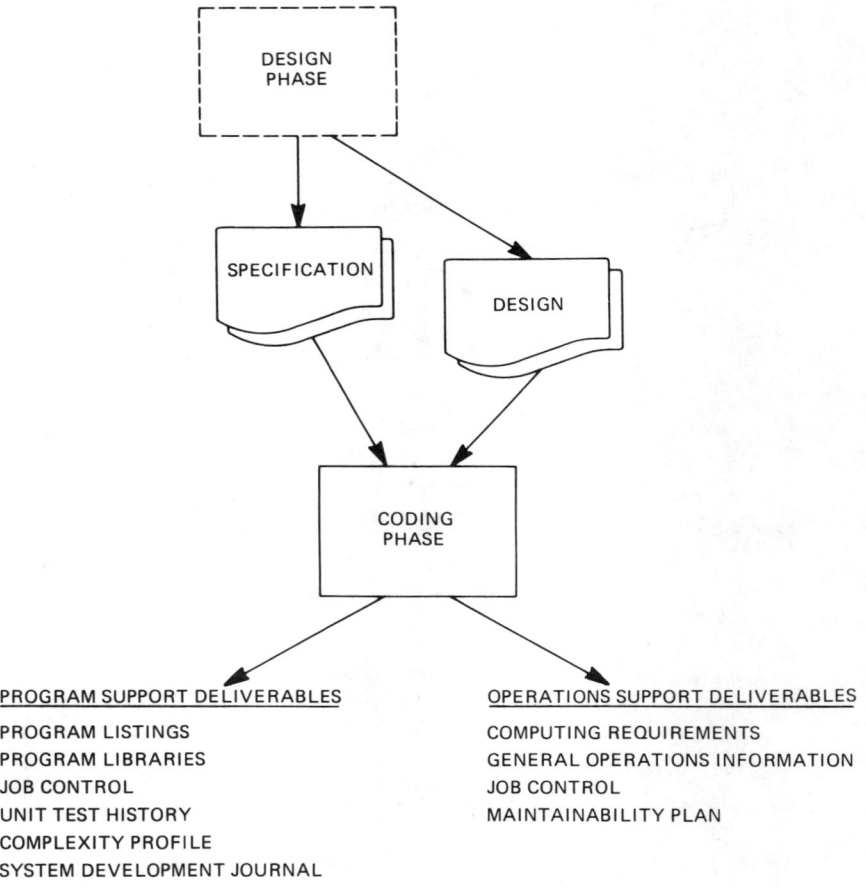

PROGRAM SUPPORT DELIVERABLES
PROGRAM LISTINGS
PROGRAM LIBRARIES
JOB CONTROL
UNIT TEST HISTORY
COMPLEXITY PROFILE
SYSTEM DEVELOPMENT JOURNAL

OPERATIONS SUPPORT DELIVERABLES
COMPUTING REQUIREMENTS
GENERAL OPERATIONS INFORMATION
JOB CONTROL
MAINTAINABILITY PLAN

Fig. 5.8.   Coding phase deliverables.

Freeze-points occur concurrently with check-points (see Table 5.9). At a freeze-point, the software product deliverables and documentation produced to that point are "frozen" and can be modified only through a formal change control procedure or a formal transition at

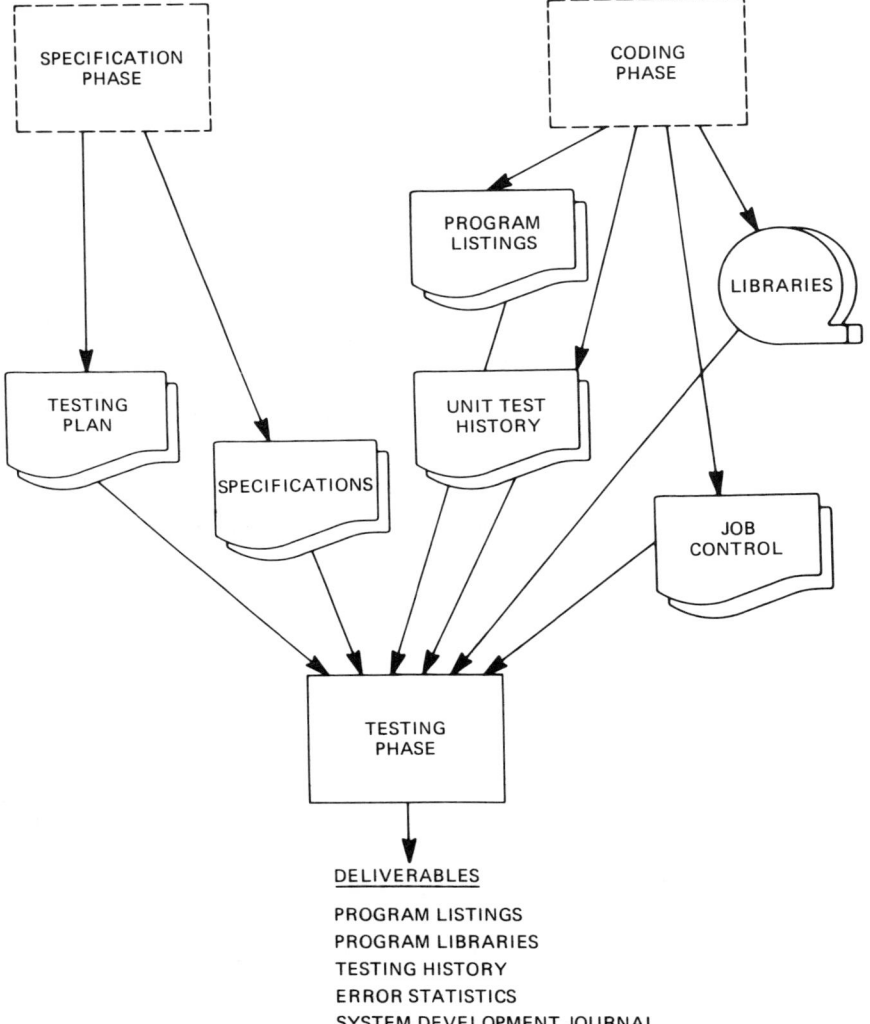

Fig. 5.9. Testing phase deliverables.

the next check-point/freeze-point. Freezing the project serves as the basis of common understanding across the entire project population —analysts, programmers, testers, users, maintainers, and management—and allows the project to proceed in a coordinated fashion with everyone working on the same software. As an example, consider the Specification Phase Check-point Review occurring at the end of the specification phase. Freezing the specifications at this point means no changes may be made to the specifications without going through the formal change procedure. This allows the designers to develop the design while preparations for the other life cycles phases, such as the test phase and the operations and maintenance phase, are made. When a change must be made to the specification, the formal change procedure ensures that all phase groups, the management, and the user are notified and then the necessary adjustments can be made. We discuss the change procedure in more detail in Section 5.4.

The Check-point review is summarized in Table 5.8.

5.3.2.3 Introduction Reviews. *Introduction reviews* are held at the beginning of each project development phase for the following purposes:

- To review the function/objective of this development phase
- To present individual responsibilities and assignments for the phase
- To examine the input to the phase
- To identify potential problems and assign them for investigation

The introduction review is conducted by the phase chief and is attended by the team members responsible for executing that development phase. The format for the review is the structured walkthrough. Materials to be reviewed during an introduction review include the project objectives, priorities, schedule, and the various software deliverables specified in Fig. 5.6–5.9 and used as input for this development phase.

The introduction review is an excellent point at which to "sell the project" to the team, as we discussed in Chapter 2. When discussing project goals and priorities, the phase chief can explain the importance of each team member's contribution to the project. He can explain

CONTROLLING SOFTWARE DEVELOPMENT 115

Table 5.8. Check-point Review Summary.

CHECK-POINT	REVIEWEE	REVIEWERS	MATERIAL TO BE REVIEWED	CONTROL DOCUMENTS
Requirements Analysis Phase	Requirements Phase Chief	Project Leader/Co-Leader, Phase Chiefs, User Liaison, Maintainer	Requirements, Schedule, Constraints	Requirements Phase Acceptance Form, Incident Reports
Specification Phase	Specification Phase Chief	Project Leader/Co-Leader, Phase Chiefs, User Liaison, Maintainer, Audit Group	Specifications, Schedule, Test Plan	Specification Phase Acceptance Form, Incident Reports
Design Phase	Design Phase Chief	Project Leader/Co-Leader, Phase Chiefs, User Liaison, Maintainer, Audit Group	Design Approach, Design, Schedule, Implementation Plan, Operation and Maintenance Support Plan	Design Phase Acceptance Form, Incident Reports
Coding Phase	Coding Phase Chief	Project Leader/Co-Leader, Phase Chiefs, User Liaison, Maintainer, Audit Group	Code, System Documentation, Unit Test Results, Complexity Profile	Coding Phase Acceptance Form, Incident Reports
Testing Phase	Testing Phase Chief	Project Leader/Co-Leader, Phase Chiefs, User Liaison, Maintainer, Audit Group	Test Results, User Documentation, System Documentation, Operation and Maintenance Documentation	Testing Phase Acceptance Form, Incident Reports

Table 5.9. Check-Points and Freeze-Points.

CHECK-POINT	FREEZE-POINT	DELIVERABLES AND DOCUMENTATION FROZEN
Requirements Analysis Phase	x	Requirements
Specification Phase	x	Requirements Specifications Test Plan Project Schedule
Design Phase	x	Requirements Specifications Design Contingency Plan Test Plan
Coding Phase	x	Requirements Specifications Design Contingency Plan Test Plan Source Code and Documentation
Testing Phase	x	Requirements Specifications Design Source Code and Documentation Operation Documentation User Documentation

the impact of the new system on the total organization, and the technical challenges and experience offered to the team members as well as possible promotion paths for high performers. Such information may help create a team spirit and improve chances for project success.

An Introduction Review form (see Table 5.10) should be filled out by the phase chief at the completion of the introduction review. It contains a checklist of all input items to be received and reviewed and a list of investigation assignments for potential problems identified during the walk-through. It is signed by the phase chief and all the walk-through participants to signify their approval of the deliverables (with exceptions noted) and their acceptance of the responsibility for completing that project phase. The signed Introduction Review form becomes a permanent project control document (see Section 5.3.4).

Potential problems identified during the walk-through should be reported by the recording secretary on Incident Report forms and given to the phase chief. It is the responsibility of the phase chief to see that these problems are investigated and that their status is reported to the project leader during status meetings (see Section 5.3.3).

A summary of the Introduction Review is given in Table 5.11.

5.3.3 Status Reporting

5.3.3.1 Status Reporting Rules. Formal status reporting is used as a mechanism for project control. Its structure is formalized to ensure that timely and relevant information will be made available to all levels of management throughout the project. The purpose of status reporting is to accomplish the following:

- Update the project schedule. (Examine what is falling behind schedule, why and what to do about it.)
- Discuss and resolve problems.
- Assess system quality and adherence to standards.
- Make and/or modify assignments.
- Exchange general project news and comments.

During a status meeting, the manager can learn about attitudes and feelings of the various team members toward the project that are difficult to detect in a written status report. As we learned in Chapter 2 from the GIRG project, the team attitude can affect the success of a project. Assessing team enthusiasm and support for the project is

Table 5.10. Introduction Checklist Review.

```
                            Table 5.10
                    Introduction Checklist Review


APPLICATION: _____ PROGRAM: _____
SUBROUTINE/MODULE NUMBER: _____
DEVELOPMENT PHASE: _____

                          INPUT CHECKLIST

    _____ System Requirements & Constraints    _____ Program Listings
    _____ Project Objectives, Priorities       _____ Program Libraries
    _____ Project Schedule                     _____ Program Documentation
    _____ System Specification                 _____ Unit Test History
    _____ Design Documents                     _____ Complexity Profile
    _____ Test Plan                            _____ Job Control
    _____ Test Cases, Data and Expected Results

                          MISSING INPUT
    _____
    _____
    _____
    _____

                 PROBLEM INVESTIGATION ASSIGNMENTS
    PROBLEM: _____ ASSIGNED TO: _____
             _____              _____
             _____              _____
             _____              _____

    Reviewee:  _____  Date: _____

    Reviewers: _____  Date: _____
               _____        _____
               _____        _____
```

Table 5.11. Introduction Review Summary.

INTRODUCTION	REVIEWEE	REVIEWERS	INPUT REVIEWED	CONTROL DOCUMENTS
Requirements Phase	Requirements Phase Chief	System Analysts, User Liaison, Maintainer	Project Objectives, Priorities, Constraints	Introduction Review Form, Incident Reports
Specification Phase	Specification Phase Chief	System Analysts, User Liaison, Maintainer	System Requirements, Project Priorities, Objectives, Schedule, Constraints	Introduction Review Form, Incident Reports
Design Phase	Design Phase Chief	Design Analysts, User Liaison, Maintainer	System Requirements, Project Constraints, Schedule, Specifications, Test Plan	Introduction Review Form, Incident Reports
Coding Phase	Coding Phase Chief	Programmers, Maintainer	Schedule, Specifications, Design, Test Plan	Introduction Review Form, Incident Reports
Testing Phase	Testing Phase Chief	Testers, User Liaison, Maintainer	Specifications, Schedule, Test Plan, Test Cases, Data, and Expected Results, Code, Complexity Profile, Unit Test History, Job Control	Incident Reports, Introduction Review Form

an essential part of an accurate picture of project status. In an attempt to detect problems early and to provide planned, nonreactionary direction for a team, the manager should actively solicit comments, complaints, and suggestions from the team. Of course, the manager should never allow a status meeting to degenerate into a pointless attack on "the establishment," but rather must always display a positive attitude toward the project, the user, upper management, and the company as a whole while still remaining sympathetic to subordinates' viewpoints. Otherwise, the team may lose interest in the project and may lose trust in the company. The manager should view each status meeting as an opportunity to break down the isolated feeling of project teams by bringing to the meeting news of the company, the department, and other teams, and a report that the team efforts and needs are recognized and understood by management.

Recall that earlier in the chapter we defined four basic project management levels:

1. Upper management
2. Project administrator
3. Project leader
4. Phase chief

The rules for status reporting apply to all four project management levels and include the following:

1. Status meetings are held on a periodic basis (determined by the project management level) at a regular time for a fixed period of one hour.
2. Status meetings are conducted by the person responsible for that management level and are attended by the staff reporting directly to that manager.
3. Every status meeting has a fixed agenda:
    - Update actual project schedule, discussing any differences arising between the estimated and actual schedule.
    - Discuss problems affecting other project tasks and/or the schedule.
    - Make assignments.
    - Discuss overall project news and team comments.

CONTROLLING SOFTWARE DEVELOPMENT   121

4. Each attendant comes to the status meeting with prepared copies of all required control documents to be submitted to his manager.
5. Problems are reported on Incident Report forms.
6. A status report summarizing the project status at that level is written by the manager who conducted the meeting and is submitted to his immediate manager. The status report should highlight:
   - schedule changes and their ramifications on other parts of the project and other project groups
   - problems discovered and problems solved.
7. Problems that do not concern the whole group should not be discussed during the status meeting. Such problems should be brought to the manager's attention and a time should be arranged when they can be discussed.

Each management level status reporting structure is discussed further in the sections that follow.

5.3.3.2 Phase Chief Level Status Reporting. Each project phase chief conducts status reporting meetings on a weekly basis with all his immediate subordinates present. The meetings follow the rules outlined in Section 5.3.3.1. Control documents submitted by each subordinate include:

- Weekly time distribution sheets (may use an automated time reporting system)
- Incident reports
- Change requests (see Section 5.4)

During the meeting, the schedule is updated, problems are discussed, and assignments are made. The phase chief has the authority to settle disputes or problems that do not affect other parts of the project. If a problem or a dispute does affect other parts of the project, the phase chief must notify his leader of the problem documented on an Incident Report or Change Request form.

The status meeting is held prior to the weekly status meeting of the pnase chief with his project leader. The phase chief prepares a written summary report of this status meeting to be submitted at the weekly project leader status meeting.

5.3.3.3 Project Leader Level Status Reporting. Each project leader conducts weekly status meetings with all his immediate subordinates present. The meetings follow the rules outlined in Section 5.3.3.1. Control documents submitted by each subordinate at the meeting include:

- Weekly time distribution reports from the team
- Unresolved Incident Reports
- Change Requests

The project leader has the authority to settle disputes and problems among phase chiefs provided these problems do not affect the tasks of other project leaders. In such cases, the problems should be documented on Incident Report forms and submitted to the project administrator for resolution. The project leader prepares a summary status report highlighting project status and problems. This report is submitted at the semimonthly project administrator status meeting.

5.3.3.4 Project Administrator Level Status Reporting. The project administrator conducts semimonthly status meetings with all project leaders. The meetings follow the rules outlined in Section 5.3.3.1. Control documents prepared and submitted by each project manager include:

- Weekly time distribution sheets from the team (An automated time reporting system may be used.)
- Unresolved Incident Reports
- Change Requests

The project administrator has the authority to settle all disputes and/or problems among the project leaders provided the scope, the intent, or the cost of the project are not changed. In such cases, these problems should be reported to upper management for resolution. Following each project administrator status meeting, the project administrator submits a written summary status report discussing project status and problems to upper management.

5.3.4 Control Documents

Control documents are used to keep the project visible to all management levels (see Fig. 5.10). They are a management tool for monitoring the project schedule, cost, and problems, and for recording project history. Since the people who develop, support, and use the software are likely to change many times during the software life cycle, it is very important to record *in writing* all control information about the project. Also, control documents represent a commitment from project participants. Signing a control document represents an approval of certain software product deliverables or an acceptance of certain project responsibilities on the part of the signatory.

There are six types of written control documents:

1. Introduction Review document—
   Used to record the inputs to a project phase and to make assignments.
2. Check-point Review document—
   Used to record the deliverables produced by a project phase.
3. Schedule—
   Used to track the actual project schedule against the expected project schedule.
4. Incident Report document—
   Used to record project problems.
5. Change Request document—
   Used to record project change requests.
6. Written Status reports—
   Used to summarize for each management level the project status.

Use of these documents is discussed throughout the chapter.

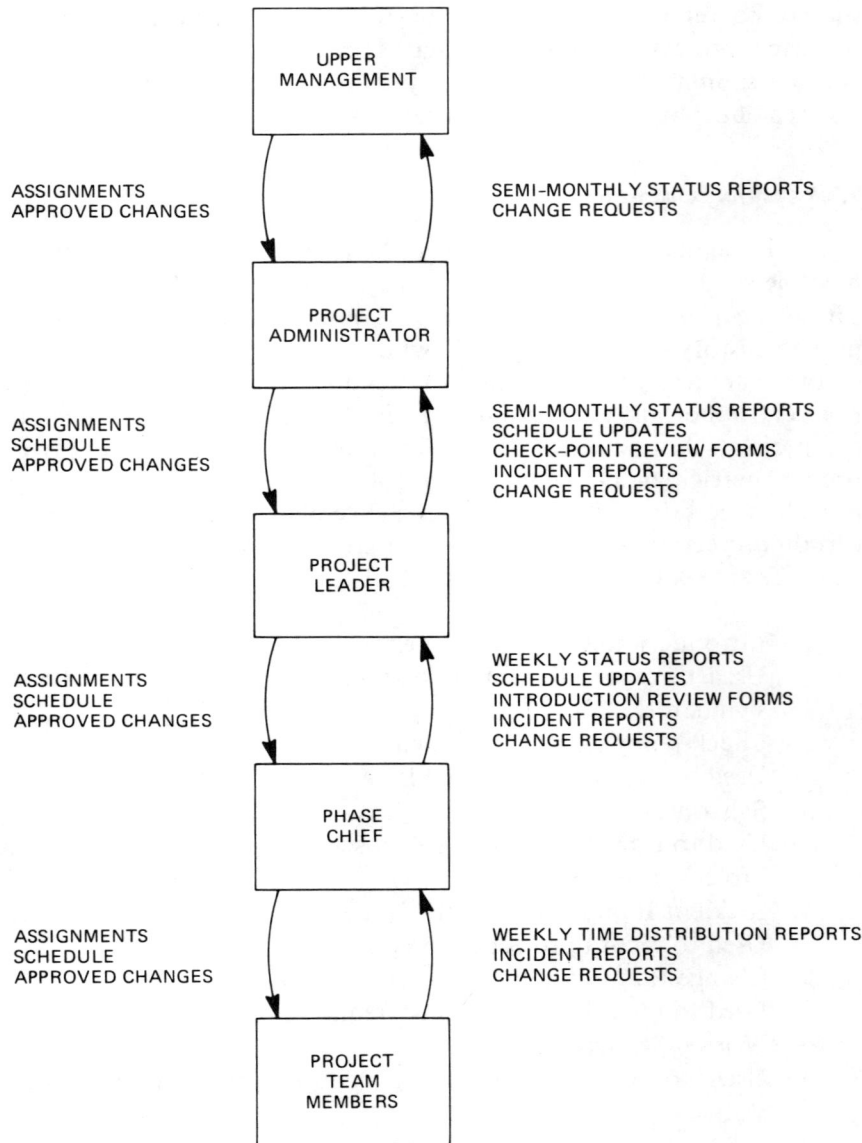

Fig. 5.10. Written control documents.

5.3.5 System Development Journal

To understand a software system it is necessary to understand how the software was developed as well as what was developed. Recording the system development philosophy, the decision-making strategies used, and the reasons for selecting particular design alternatives makes the software more understandable, especially as time goes on. In Chapter 3, we suggested that a System Development Journal containing the following information be kept:

- Project objectives
- Project priorities
- Basic assumptions
- Development philosophy
- Design dilemmas and/or trade-offs
- Change requirements
- System problem areas and weak-points

The System Development Journal should be considered a record accessible to the project team members, manangement and the system maintainer. Copies of the following control documents should be included in the *System Development Journal:*

- Check-point Review documents
- Information Review documents
- Change Requests with approval
- Schedule (Estimated and Actual)
- Incident Reports affecting multiple project phase groups or teams

5.4 CHANGE CONTROL

5.4.1 Changes

Because developing a large software system is a complex task involving many activities and many people, changes will undoubtedly occur throughout system evolution. Changes occur as the user learns more about this new system and begins to see more possibilities for its application if certain modifications are made. Changes occur as errors, oversights and implementation inefficiencies are discovered by the developers. They also occur as part of maintaining a system throughout its production life.

In this chapter, we address only the first two types of changes—changes that occur during system development. These changes can be classified into three kinds:

1. Requirements changes
2. Specification changes
3. Coding changes

It is essential to project survival that management control these kinds of changes. If not, it will be impossible for project teams to be certain that they are working with the latest version of the software, and it will be impossible for management to track the progress of a project with unknown scope. A formal change control mechanism is necessary for management to control development changes.

Not all changes occurring during system development fall under the control of the formal change control mechanism. If they did, the paper work would be unwieldy. Changes that

- occur during a development phase before its freeze-point,
- do not affect any previously frozen development phase, and
- do not change the scope, intent, or cost estimates for the project

do *not* fall under the formal change control mechanism. For example, many changes to the specifications will occur during the specification phase. This is a normal part of software development. Unless these changes modify the scope of the project, they are not included in the formal change control process. They do, however, fall under the control and guidance of the Specification Phase Chief. As a second example, many changes to the code will occur during the coding phase as the programmers find better ways to implement the specifications and find errors during unit testing. Unless these changes require a change to the design specifications, they should not be subject to the formal change control process. However, unit testing errors whose correction requires modifying the code for multiple modules should be brought to the attention of the Coding Phase Chief during the weekly status meeting.

Changes that *do* fall under the formal change control mechanism are changes that

- affect the previous development phase(s) that have been frozen, or
- affect more than one development phase that is currently underway (since development phases may proceed in parallel).

For example if, during coding, a specification change is requested to correct an error or to accommodate a user request, this change is subject to the formal change process before it can be incorporated into the software. This will ensure that all phase groups will be informed of the change and will have the opportunity to make necessary adjustments. As a second example, if during integration or system testing a change is required to the design to correct an error, this change is subject to the formal change process. Again, this will ensure that all phase groups will be informed of the change.

5.4.2 Change Control Mechanism

The change control mechanism can be used to control the three kinds of software development changes:

- Requirements changes
- Specification changes
- Code changes

A *requirement change* is defined as a modification to the Requirements document after it has been frozen; a *specification change* is defined as a modification to the Specification document after it has been frozen; a *code change* is defined as a modification to the source code after it has been frozen.

Such changes must be formally requested and approved before they are incorporated into the system. The procedure is as follows:

1. The change must be documented on a Change Request form by the requester (see Table 5.12).
2. The Change Request form is submitted by the requester at the status meeting to his immediate manager if he is a member of the development team. Users submit change requests to the user liaison.
3. The manager has the authority to assess the validity of any changes requested by his subordinates. A subordinate may request that his manager's decision be reviewed by the next level manager.
4. Lower-level managers pass all change requests with recommendations to their project leader.
5. At each project leader status meeting, all outstanding change requests are reviewed. Each change request should have been previously reviewed by the manager of the requester and should include a recommendation for accepting or rejecting the change.
6. Specification changes and code changes that do *not* modify the project scope or cost or delay the project schedule may be approved at the project leader status meetings. The project leader has the authority to settle disputes among phase chiefs concerning these types of changes.
7. Specification changes and code changes that *do* modify the project scope, intent or cost or delay the project schedule must be approved by the project administrator. Also, all requirement changes must be approved by the project administrator. Such change requests along with recommendations from the project leader and the phase chief(s) should be submitted to the project administrator for his approval at status meetings.
8. Emergency change requests that require immediate review and approval should be submitted by the requester to his manager without delay.
9. The implementation of approved changes falls under the authority of the project leader.

Table 5.12. Change Request.

```
                           Table 5.12
                         Change Request


APPLICATION: _____ PROGRAM: _____
SUBROUTINE/MODULE NUMBER: _____
REQUESTER: _____ DATE: _____


TYPE OF CHANGE
    _____ Requirement
    _____ Specification
    _____ Code


REASON FOR CHANGE
_____
_____
_____



IMPACT TO SYSTEM
_____
_____
_____



RECOMMENDATIONS
_____
_____
_____



APPROVALS
PROJECT ADMINISTRATOR:   _____ YES     _____ NO    DATE: _____
PROJECT LEADER:          _____ YES     _____ NO    DATE: _____
PHASE CHIEF:             _____ YES     _____ NO    DATE: _____
```

10. Copies of the approved change requests should be placed in the System Development Journal. All phase chiefs should be notified in writing by the project leader of each approved change request, enabling them to make appropriate adjustments to their project tasks.

5.5 SUMMARY

In this chapter, we discussed formal project management methods for controlling all software development activities. We introduced formality as a means of dealing with the complex problems of coordinating project members, project tasks and project changes. The project management methods discussed include:

- Explicit assignment of project responsibilities based upon an extended Revised Chief Programmer Team structure
- Use of structured walk-through reviews at the introduction and completion of each project development phase to assign project responsibilities and tasks and to assess software quality
- Establishment of a status reporting structure including intra-project management levels and upper management
- Record of project events in written control documents and in a Systems Development Journal to preserve project development philosophy and decisions

The objective of these methods is to keep the software project and the software product visible throughout the development phases by providing timely and accurate project information to the software development team, to the maintainer, to management, and to the user on a periodic, scheduled basis.

Part 3
Managing Software Maintenance

Applying Software Engineering to Software Maintenance

6.1 INTRODUCTION

A major objective of this book is to present methods to meet the growing demands for more and better quality software. In Parts I and II, we studied the fundamental principles of software engineering, as applied to the software development life cycle phases, to realize our objective. In Part III, we focus on software maintenance, considering this the major thrust of the book. Because the maintenance phase dominates the software life cycle in terms of effort and costs, we cannot hope to realize our objective without presenting methods for structuring the maintenance function.

Strangely enough, software literature has for the most part neglected the subject of software maintenance. Most software discussions on cost and quality control center around the development of complete and reliable software, that is, software for which the requirements are completely and explicitly defined and implemented in error-free, well-structured code. The reasoning is that the quality introduced in the software development process will extend into the entire software life cycle, thereby reducing overall software effort and cost. The flaw in this reasoning is that it assumes the problems of software quality end with the completion of the development process, when in practice, they are just beginning because of change. We have failed to recognize that an inherent characteristic of software is its dynamic nature—its propensity to change as it is used.

Software changes occur not only as a consequence of detecting and correcting errors not discovered during testing, but also as a consequence of postponing development tasks until the maintenance phase, because of tight schedules and as a consequence of changing system requirements. As a matter of fact, a recent study shows that the majority (82 percent) of the maintenance effort is devoted to system enhancements, performance improvements, and user requests, while a much smaller portion (18 percent) is devoted to error corrections.[1] It is unrealistic to assume that requirements are permanently definable. In large software systems that require many man-years to build, user requirements will change as the user's needs change and as the user group itself changes. In some systems—such as management information systems—requirements by definition are not completely known when the system is defined. The user of an information system must have the capability to change requirements with the use of the system.

• As it is changed, the quality of a software system deteriorates because new errors are introduced as a side effect of change. For example, it has been estimated that there is a 20 to 50 percent probability of introducing an error each time the software is changed.[2] Eventually this leads to a totally degraded software system whose use is no longer practical nor cost-effective. Because maintenance personnel typically are less experienced and less familiar with the software than original software development personnel, and because state-of-the-art tools and software engineering disciplines have not been introduced to the same degree in maintenance as in new development, software quality is threatened by the maintenance process. We have not learned to handle change in the technical sense of modifying software without increasing its complexity or jeopardizing its integrity, nor in the management sense of controlling user change requests.

Many of our maintenance problems have grown out of a mistaken belief that the maintenance task is generally easier than the development task, and therefore, requires less planning, less expertise, fewer technical tools, and less management direction. On the contrary, maintenance tasks are often more difficult than new development tasks because they require working with the entire system to a greater degree, and they require reconstructing the original motivations and decision-making process of the developer. For example, when correcting an error, we must first study the entire system to determine all portions of the code contributing to the problem; next we must determine how to modify the code to correct the problem; and then we again must study the entire system to assess the ramification of the modifications. On the other hand, much of the new development effort is confined to the internals of particular system subcomponents.

If we continue to address software quality and cost problems as only a production issue we will find that although we improve the quality of the software we produce, software costs will continue to soar and software life expectancy will decrease. We will find that our maintenance problems will be further compounded by the sheer number of systems to be maintained and by the increasing size and complexity of new systems. We must learn how to build software systems that can tolerate change and we must learn how to adapt the software engineering discipline used in software development to the maintenance function.

In this book, our approach to addressing these maintenance issues is summarized by the following activities:

- Inclusion of quality control standards and audits in the development process to ensure the quality of software maintainability
- Inclusion of the maintainer in the development process to reduce the maintenance learning curve
- Adaptation of the software engineering discipline used to improve the development process to the maintenance function
- Structuring of the maintenance organization to make the maintenance process more visible to management and more amenable to management controls
- Establishment of communication channels among the developer, the user, and the maintainer to control user requests and to anticipate user needs

In Part II, we presented guidelines for each software development phase to ensure the quality of maintainability in a software system. We also discussed the participation of the system maintainer in the development process. In Part III, we discuss the application of the software engineering discipline to the software maintenance function.

Part III consists of two chapters. In Chapter 6, we structure the maintenance process into a well-defined, step-by-step process that is directed by software engineering disciplines and quality control audits.

In Chapter 7, we address the management problems of the maintenance process. We define an organizational structure for the maintenance staff and a software change request procedure.

6.2 MAINTENANCE

Maintenance is the function of keeping software in an operational mode. The maintenance function involves correcting software errors in the specifications, design, code, and performance requirements; and modifying the software to comply with user requests, changes in the operating environment, and data requirements.

In our discussion of maintenance, we assume that maintenance is performed as a separate activity from new development and redevelopment efforts. Maintenance activities are based upon the design specifications of the installed production version of a software system, whereas development and redevelopment activities are based upon a revision to the design specifications. Also, we assume that the maintenance personnel are a separate group from the development personnel.

We define the *maintenance process* as including four basic steps[3] (see Fig. 6.1):

1. Understand the software.
2. Identify the modification objective and the modification approach.
3. Implement the modification.
4. Revalidate the software.

Since performing the maintenance function presupposes a knowledge of the software—its functional objective, its internal structure and its operational requirements—the first step in the maintenance process is to gain an understanding of the software. During the second step, a determination as to why the software must be modified and a plan for modifying the software—including the estimated effort, schedule, cost, specification, design, and code alterations, and a revalidation plan—are made. Next, the software and its related documentation are modified according to the modification plan. Finally, the software is tested to reaffirm its ability to comply to system specifications, performance requirements, and quality control standards.

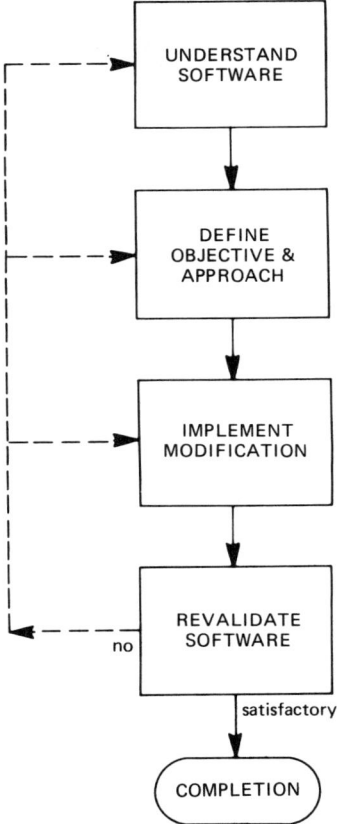

Fig. 6.1. The maintenance process.

If the result of this step is unsatisfactory, the previous maintenance steps are repeated until the software has been successfully modified.

Frequently cited problem areas in performing the maintenance process include:[4]

- Quality of the original software
- Quality of documentation
- Limited test resources
- High learning curve due to the complexity of the software

In the rest of the chapter, we shall address these problem areas as part of our discussion of applying the software engineering discipline to the maintenance process.

6.3 PERFORMING MAINTENANCE

6.3.1 The Basic Ingredients

Recall from Chapter 2 that there are three basic ingredients necessary to ensure the success of a software development effort:

- Technical tools
- Technical expertise
- Management techniques

These ingredients are also fundamental to the maintenance process. Just as in software development, ignoring the importance of these ingredients can greatly increase the risk of failure in a maintenance effort. What can the maintainer do to provide the basic ingredients necessary for successfully performing the maintenance function?

First, we consider the need for technical tools. Our argument is that the need for state-of-the-art technical tools is as great in maintenance as in development and redevelopment activities because of the difficulty of the maintenance task. In the past, poor tools such as inadequate computer test time and inadequate on-line debugging aids have impaired the maintenance function. The technical tools provided to the developer should also be provided to the maintainer.

For example, sophisiticated development tools such as environmental and interface simulators, that have been viewed as strictly development tools to be discarded at system completion, should be made available to the maintainer. These tools and other special-purpose tools can help streamline the maintenance function, and their cost can be quickly justified by the reduction of ongoing maintenance costs. The maintainer should include the tools necessary to support a software system in the set of maintainability criteria for acceptance of a software system into the operation and maintenance phase (see Chapter 3, Section 3.3.7). As a guideline, the following should be included in the list of maintenance tools:[5]

- Spare computing capacity for maintenance tasks even under the worst caseload situations
- A test environment that is capable of simulating an operational environment
- Test data generators and verifiers
- Program support libraries
- On-line diagnostic programs offering trace, snap, dump, inspect, and change capabilities
- Source code auditors for structure checking

Next, we consider the need for technical expertise. Repeating our argument that maintaining a software system is generally very difficult, the software maintainer should possess a high level of technical expertise. This, of course, is contrary to the traditional approach of placing trainees in the maintenance area to "learn the business." The result of this approach has been an accelerated degradation of costly software. Instead, we suggest an alternative approach of applying the software engineering guideline: Use the best people.[7] Senior, not junior, personnel should form the nucleus of the maintenance group. The maintainer should not only be an experienced software engineer, but should also have perfected the skills for determining the cause of malfunctions and the ramifications of change and have demonstrated an indepth knowledge of the application area and user needs. The training for a software maintainer should be broader than that for a software developer. Besides being knowledgeable in the state-of-the-art software engineering principles and methods, the maintainer should receive training in application areas, in technological trends, and in statistical analysis. Knowledge of the application area in terms of how the software is being used, what functions are most useful, characteristics of the user groups, additional related applications, and government and/or industry regulations for the application area may help the maintainer better anticipate changes. Knowledge of technical trends in hardware and software advances may help the maintainer anticipate how the software must change to continue to be cost-effective. Knowledge of statistical analysis techniques such as regression analysis and hypothesis testing may help the maintainer identify relationships between maintainability qualities and error tendencies, thereby extending the life expectancy of expensive software systems. In large groups, maintenance specialization should be encouraged. For example. a maintainer may specialize in a particular application area. We discuss the organization of the maintenance staff in Chapter 7.

Finally, we consider the need for management techniques. Again we borrow suggestions for structuring the maintenance process from our software development experience. As in development activities, management problems in maintenance have become more serious than technical problems due to the complexity of software systems and the continual need for change.[6] The need for planned, nonreactionary management of the maintenance function cannot be overemphasized. Fundamental to such a management approach is the incorporation of the following four activities:

1. Establishment of the priorities and goals sought
2. Continued enforcement of the same standards that are used to control quality during software development
3. Documentation of the maintenance process as well as the software modifications
4. Periodic quality control audits and acceptance reviews

In Chapter 3, we learned that clearly defining project goals and priorities for a software development team increases the chances of achieving project success. This applies to maintenance efforts as well. The first step toward preserving software quality during the maintenance phase is to clearly explain this goal to the maintenance group in terms of measurable qualities and quality control standards. The quality control standards enforced during software development must continue to be enforced during maintenance. Specification, source code, change control, and documentation standards are especially important to preserving the quality of maintainability.

Also in Chapter 3, we learned that the software developer should record the software development process in the System Development Journal and that the System Development Journal should be included in the system documentation given to the system maintainer at project completion. Understanding the decision-making process is an important component in understanding a complex software system. Likewise, the maintainer should record the maintenance process in a

System Maintenance Journal containing information such as maintenance objectives, priorities, basic assumptions, change philosophy, problems, and so forth. Understanding the thought process behind the modifications is key to understanding what was modified.

For each modification made to a software system, the following information should be recorded in the System Maintenance Journal:

- Date modification began and date completed
- Reason for making modification
- Name of each program changed and program change level number
- For each program changed, record:
  — Number of hours spent making change
  — Number of statements changed
  — Number of modules changed
  — Languages used
- Personnel assigned to modification task
- Special problems encountered
- Date modification became effective

In structuring software development, we followed the software engineering principle: Manage a software project using a sequential life cycle plan.[8] Following this principle meant that the next software development phase was not begun until the previous phase met a set of acceptance criteria including quality control standards. Including audit steps in the maintenance process will allow management to control the maintenance function and to become informed of problems as soon as possible. We suggest two types of audit reviews:

1. An audit review of each modification to ensure that modifications comply with standards and that software quality has been preserved.
2. A periodic audit review of the software system to ensure that software quality remains at an acceptable level during the maintenance phase.

6.3.2 Guidelines for Software Maintenance

In Chapter 1 we presented a set of general software engineering guidelines. We now adapt these guidelines to the maintenance function. They serve as the basis of our structured approach to performing maintenance. We explain this approach further in the sections that follow.

GUIDELINES FOR SOFTWARE MAINTENANCE

1. Technical Guidelines
   1.1 Use state-of-the-art tools such as well-engineered operating systems, code auditors, cross reference generators, documentation generators, test data generators, on-line diagnostic programs, source management systems, etc.
   1.2 Use structured programming.
   1.3 Use a combination top-down/bottom-up design approach.
   1.4 Develop a revalidation plan as part of the modification plan.
   1.5 Use high-order languages.
   1.6 Strive for machine independence and code compatibility with language standards and software development standards.
   1.7 Opt for the quality of maintainability over the quality of efficiency.
   1.8 Keep a repository of common functions to be used in coding modifications.
   1.9 Survey successful software engineering techniques and adapt them for use in the maintenance environment.
2. Product Control Guidelines
   2.1 Define maintenance tasks in terms of required, optional, and future requirements.
   2.2 Modify software with maintainability in mind.
   2.3 Opt for simplicity and clarity over completeness.
   2.4 Perform periodic software product quality control reviews.
   2.5 Involve the user in reviews.
   2.6 Update user documentation.
   2.7 Update system documentation.

3. Project Control Guidelines
   3.1 Develop a maintenance support plan and use it to manage the maintenance process.
   3.2 Define explicitly maintenance goals and priorities for the maintenance group.
   3.3 Produce clear, concise statements of user requirements to be reviewed periodically with the user.
   3.4 Use fewer and better people to staff the maintenance group.
   3.5 Maintain clear accountability of each individual member of the maintenance group, enabling maintainers to gage their performance.
   3.6 Set up career paths, salary scales, and benefits to reward high performers.
   3.7 Do not use automated tools and software engineering techniques as a substitute for good management.
   3.8 Develop program libraries for maintenance management.
   3.9 Evaluate maintenance success in terms of its goals.

6.3.3 Understanding a Software System

In Chapter 3, we began discussing the system maintainer's need to understand the software to be supported. This was one reason for our stressing the active participation of the system maintainer in the software development process. Because of hardware advances, the trend is to develop larger and more sophisticated software systems requiring greater preparation time to learn about and to plan for support facilities, support tools, and support personnel. We suggested that the maintainer interact with the developer to learn about the development approach and with the user to learn about anticipated uses of the software. We also suggested that the system maintainer participate in the software development process by attending introduction reviews at the beginning of each development phase and check-point reviews at the completion of each development phase (see Chapter 5, Section 5.3.2) and by defining maintainability standards to be met for system acceptance into the operation and maintenance phase (see Chapter 3, Section 3.3.7). Waiting until the maintenance phase to develop a maintenance plan is likely to increase the cost of supporting

software. The Maintenance Support Plan should be developed during software development and should contain provisions for the following.
1. Software failure reporting and correction procedures
2. Change request and implementation procedures
3. Maintainability and general quality control protection plan
4. Revalidation procedures including test cases, test data and test results
5. Documentation update procedure
6. Support requirements
   — Equipment configuration
   — Technical tools
   — Personnel requirements
   — User interface and support
   — Test bed resources and test facilities
   — User manuals and operation manuals
   — System documents including requirements, specifications, design, System Development Journal, Complexity Profile and Test History
   — Source code listings and libraries
   — Source management libraries
7. New Release procedure

Part of developing a Maintenence Support Plan is determining the effort needed to support the software. In the past, we have experienced great difficulty in accurately estimating the time and the manpower effort required to perform software tasks. Most estimation errors result from underestimates of size (in object or source code instructions). In a study by the Doty team, size estimate errors in software development tasks were as high as 200 percent in the problem definition phase, 75 percent in the preliminary design phase and 50 percent through the remainder of development.[9]

Typically, estimates for software development are based on previous experiences—if possible, using a similar application developed previously in the same organization. This approach combines macro and micro estimating techniques in that the task is viewed as a whole and also as a set of subtasks whose scopes can be individually estimated.

The following steps are performed in arriving at the estimate:[10]

1. Comparing the project to previous projects.
2. Dividing the project into units, and comparing units.
3. Scheduling work by month and estimate of manpower resources by month.

Manpower resources include programmer (80 percent), management (13 percent), and support personnel (7 percent).[11]

Several factors are considered in making the estimate:[12]

1. Type of application (e.g., control programs, scientific applications, business applications, utility programs)
2. Number of people to be assigned to the task
3. Skill level of the people assigned to the task
4. Technical tools available
5. Number of interfaces with other groups and other software systems
6. Size of the task (in object or source instructions)
7. Difficulty of task.

In studies of programming rates achieved in previous projects, it appears that the type of application influences the programming rate. For example, the programming rates reported for control program development projects (600 statements per man-year) have been much lower than those reported for business application development projects (6000 statements per man-year).[13]

The number of people assigned to a task affects the length of time needed to complete the task. Adding more people should shorten the time needed to perform the task. However, this is true only to a certain point. According to Brooks, n workers generate $n(n-1)/2$ interfaces across which communication may be necessary to successfully and correctly complete the task. Because communication requires time, in every task there is a point at which the overhead due to communications outweighs the benefits of adding another person.[14]

Also, the skill level of the people assigned to the task affects the time needed to complete the task. A strong leader is often able to accelerate the project pace and complete the task more quickly.

Further, the technical tools available may affect the time needed to complete the task. Studies have shown that the most important technical factor influencing programmer productivity is the throughput of the test bed computer facility.[15] When an on-line program development and testing environment with good response time is provided instead of a batch environment that is primarily devoted to executing production jobs, a very large increase in the productivity rate has been observed. Also, it has been observed that practicing improved methods of software engineering increases productivity rates.

Obviously, the size of the task affects the estimate of time and manpower needed. When estimating size, a micro approach is frequently used. The system is divided into units (e.g., programs, subprograms, modules). An average unit size is determined, again based on previous experience, and then the size of the task is estimated as the sum of the sizes of each unit. Also, a determination of which units are independent of one another and may be developed in parallel is made. This helps identify the maximum number of people that can concurrently work on the task.

The difficulty of the task is directly related to its size and to the type of application, and indirectly related to the development time. In addition, the difficulty of the task is affected by the interdependence of the software system with other systems. For example, Putnam[16] has defined three levels of difficulty:

1. Most difficult: new software systems that must interact within a total management information system structure
2. Medium difficulty: new standalone software system
3. Least difficult: rewrite of an existing system using much existing code

Also, studies conducted by Putnam[17] revealed a relationship between difficulty and certain software system attributes such as the number of subprograms, the number of files, and the number of reports. For example, the more files defined for the system, the more difficult the task becomes.

The estimating approach discussed above applies to software development activities. Can we adopt it for maintenance activities as well?

In general, estimates for maintenance activities should also be based upon previous experiences. Besides reviewing previous maintenance tasks, we should study the source code, the System Development Journal, the Complexity Profile and the Test History for the system to be maintained.

First, the maintainer should perform code inspections to check for compliance to coding standards. Code that deviates from the standards will probably be more difficult to maintain since its style is not as familiar to the maintenance group. Ideally, of course, management controls should force the developer to comply with standards as part of system acceptance.

Second, the maintainer should study the Complexity Profile (see Table 6.1) to identify portions of the system that exceed complexity guideline limits. For example, modules containing more than ten compares will probably require more effort to modify than modules containing fewer compares. Also, the maintainer should review the Test History (see Table 6.2). It has been noted in the literature that the code in which more errors were discovered in testing is likely to be the code in which more errors occur during maintenance.[18] These portions of the software will probably require greater maintenance support than less error-prone portions.

Further, the maintainer should review with the developer and the user any system functions that were not implemented during development because of scheduling problems. It should be decided who is to implement these functions and what is a realistic schedule and manpower estimate for their implementation.

Finally, the maintainer should perform software change exercises to determine how easily the software can be modified. The results of these exercises along with the Complexity Profile and Test History can serve as the basis for making personnel and schedule estimates on future software changes.

The seven factors considered in estimating the effort for a software development task should be considered when estimating the effort

Table 6.1. Complexity Profile.

- Size of Program
- Number of Modules in Program
- Number of Variables in Program
- Number of Global Variables in Program
- Average Module Size (In statements)
- Average Number of Compares per Module
- Average Number of Modules Accessing a Global Variable
- List of Common Modules
- List of Modules that Access More than the Average Number of Global Variables
- List of Modules that Exceed the Module Size Limit of 50 statements or Exceed the Module Compare Limit of 10 Compares

required to perform a maintenance task. Also, the number of the versions of the software system that are to be maintained should be included for consideration since multiple current versions can greatly escalate the effort required to perform maintenance tasks.

Special caution should be used when estimating maintenance activities because of the ripple effect. The ripple effect is a side-effect of modifying software that occurs when a change to one part of a software system affects other parts of the system.[19] Because of the ripple effect, the size of a maintenance task does not simply include the number of lines of code to be deleted, added, or replaced to implement the change, but also must include other parts of the software system that must be modified to preserve software correctness and efficiency. When estimating a maintenance task, all parts of the system affected by the change may not be immediately apparent.

In addition to increasing size, the ripple effect can also increase difficulty. The more interrelated the components of the system, the greater the ripple effect and the greater the difficulty of performing the task.

Table 6.2. Program Test History.

Unit Test History

- Number of Modules Unit Tested
- Average Number of Unit Tests Executed per Module
- Number of Errors Discovered during Testing
- Average Number of Errors Discovered in a Module (UAEM)
- Total Number of Statements Modified to Correct Errors
- List of Modules in which the Number of Errors Discovered Exceeds UAEM
- Types of Errors Discovered
  - Hardware Failure
  - Software Reaction to Hardware Failure
  - Coding Error
  - Design Error
  - Specification Error
- Average Length of Time to Discover and Correct an Error

Integration Test History

- Number of Integration Tests Executed
- Number of Errors Discovered during Integration Testing
- Average Number of Errors Discovered in a Module (IAEM)
- List of Modules in which the Number of Errors Discovered Exceeds IAEM
- Total Number of Statements Modified to Correct Errors
- Total Number of Modules Modified to Correct Errors
- Types of Errors Discovered
- Average Length of Time to Discover and to Correct an Error

System (Acceptance) Test History

- Number of System (Acceptance) Tests Executed
- Number of Errors Discovered during System (Acceptance) Testing
- Average Number of Errors Discovered per Module (SAEM)
- List of Modules Modified to Correct Errors
- Number of Statements Modified to Correct Errors
- Types of Errors Discovered
- Average Length of Time to Correct an Error

Complexity Correlation Figures

- List of Modules whose Complexity Exceeds the Complexity Guideline Limits and UAEM or IAEM or SAEM
- List of Modules whose Complexity Exceeds the Complexity Guideline Limits and which was Modified to Correct a System (Acceptance) Error

Estimates of the extent of the ripple effect should be included in estimates of size and difficulty and should be based on previous changes to the software system both during development phases and the maintenance phase. We discuss methods for determining and controlling the ripple effect in Section 6.3.5.

6.3.4 Determining What to Modify

In the second step of the maintenance process (see Fig. 6.1), we determine why we must modify the software and we develop a plan to achieve this objective.

We use Swanson's definition of maintenance to categorize the objective of the modification:[20]

1. Corrective Maintenance (performed to identify and to correct software failures, performance failures, and implementation failures)
2. Adaptive Maintenance (performed to adapt software to changes in the data requirements or processing environment)
3. Perfective Maintenance (performed to enhance performance, improve maintainability, or improve executing efficiency)

Based upon the survey of Lientz, Swanson, and Tompkins,[21] we expect that most of our maintenance efforts will fall into the category of Perfective Maintenance and will therefore originate as change requests rather than as responses to software failure. This means that change control is a major consideration in performing the maintenance function. We discuss this further in the next chapter.

We define the modification approach using the development phases of the software life cycle (see Fig. 6.2). For example, we expand step 2 of the maintenance process to include a requirements analysis phase, a specification phase, and a design phase. Also, a check-point review (see Chapter 5, Section 5.3.2.2) is included at the completion of this step to preserve software quality and to assess the value of making the modification. During this review, it is possible to discover that a proposed modification is *not* advantagious because of its cost or its impact on the rest of the system. In such cases, the modification should

APPLYING SOFTWARE ENGINEERING TO SOFTWARE MAINTENANCE

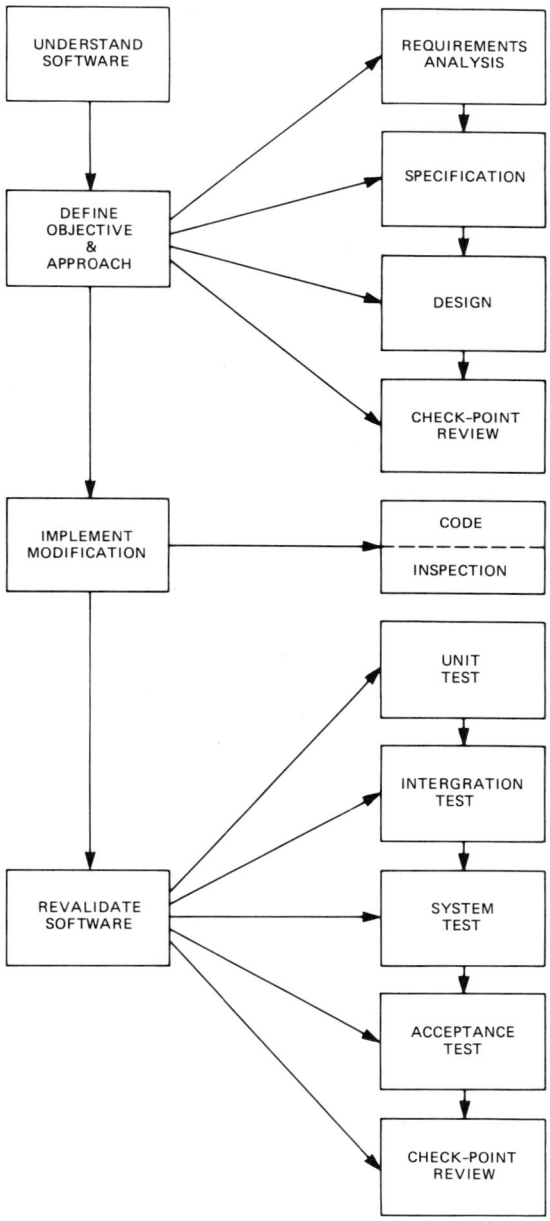

Fig. 6.2. Structuring the maintenance process.

be reconsidered before continuing to the next step of the maintenance process.

All aspects of the modification approach must be considered in the context of the existing installed software, not just in terms of the structural, human engineering, reliability, and efficiency factors that are the major considerations when developing software. The maintenance objective is to limit the effect of a modification on other parts of the installed software and on user interfaces, to avoid excessive confusion and retraining as well as to avoid compromising system integrity and quality.

During the requirements analysis phase, we define the system capabilities and the resources needed to provide the modification in the context of existing system capabilities and constraints. There are several general guidelines for performing requirements analysis for the maintenance process:

1. Determine the maintenance objective for making the modification.
2. Determine requirements for the modification with the user.
3. Define requirements in testable terms.
4. Consider changes in processing time, storage requirements, error probability, operation personnel, and other installed versions of the software.
5. Consider the effect of the modification on the human engineering aspects of the software.
6. Identify requirements in terms of contractions and/or expansions to the existing software.
7. Determine the compatibility of the modification with other software changes that are likely to occur in the future.
8. Justify the modification in terms of cost, time to implement, and risk of degrading software quality.
9. Require user and management approval of the modification requirements before proceeding to defining the specifications for the modification.

During the specification phase, we describe how the modification requirements are to be met by changing the functional specifications.

The following are general guidelines for the specification phase for the maintenance process:

1. Develop specifications for the modifications following the same standards used to develop specifications during software development.
2. Describe specifications for the modification in terms that are testable and that include test methods.
3. Identify existing programs, modules, and/or packages to be used in implementing the modification.
4. Examine the impact of the modification on the installed software and the resources needed to support the modification.
5. Require user and management approval of the specifications for the modification before proceeding to the design step.

During the design phase, we describe changes to the design algorithms and procedures. There are several general guidelines for performing the design phase for the maintenance process:

1. Examine alternative designs seeking a design for the modification that is compatible with the original design philosophy.
2. Strive for design simplicity; choose the design alternative that modifies the fewest modules, the least complex modules, and the fewest global variables.
3. Document the design and the design process for the modification following the same standards used when initially developing a design.
4. Consider the implementation feasibility of the design for the modification and its effect on the rest of the system.
5. Evaluate the generality of the design in terms of its ability to be used in various versions of the software with different operating systems and on different hardware configurations.
6. Evaluate the flexibility of the design in terms of its ability to isolate specialized functions in separate modules and to provide module interfaces that are insensitive to further changes.
7. Require user and management approval of the design for the modification before proceeding to the implementation step.

6.3.5 Implementing a Modification

During the third step of the maintenance process, we implement the modification by changing the software code. Our objective is twofold:

1. To correctly and efficiently translate the design for the modification into well-structured code
2. To minimize the impact of the modification on the rest of the software

There are several guidelines to help us achieve the first part of this objective:

1. Use structured programming and coding standards.
2. Use state-of-the-art tools such as on-line programming aids, decision tables, structure charts, etc.
3. Document all changes in the code and keep the version of the pre-modified code.
4. Duplicate code rather than create common routines for "almost duplicate" functions.
5. Code changes in a manner that will not degrade software modifiability, by not carrying machine efficiency too far.
6. Opt for human engineering over machine efficiency.
7. Record the modification process in the System Maintenance Journal.
8. Update user and operation manuals as well as system documents to reflect the modification.
9. Have a code inspection performed by someone other than the maintenance programmer who implemented the modification, to preserve software quality and compliance to standards.

We can achieve the second part of our objective to preserve software quality when modifying software by controlling the ripple effect. The *ripple effect* is defined as the phenomena by which changes to one part of a software system affect other areas of the software system.[22] This occurs because of the various interrelationships that exist

APPLYING SOFTWARE ENGINEERING TO SOFTWARE MAINTENANCE 155

between modules in a program and between programs in a system of programs. Modules (programs) are related in terms of the functions and the variables they share. For example, several modules in a program may invoke the same modules as part of performing their individual functions. When a module is invoked by more than one module in a program, it is called a *common module*. Also, several modules in a program may reference and/or change the value of the same program variable. Such a variable is called a *global variable*.

Thus, any change to a module has the potential to propagate its effect throughout the code within that module and across module boundaries into many other modules.

Not being able to determine nor to provide adjustments for all aspects of the ripple effect is a major cause of software quality deterioration during the maintenance phase.

When a change to a software system is contemplated, the modules whose code is to be rewritten—and all other modules that may indirectly be affected by these coding changes due to the ripple effect—must be determined. For example, if the calculation of the value assigned to a variable is changed in one program module, then all modules that access this variable must be examined to determine the ramification of this change on their code. Besides directly affecting this variable, the change may indirectly affect other variables.

Therefore, the effort and the difficulty of implementing the change is not simply a matter of rewriting the necessary code to implement the change, but also must include an examination of other parts of the system to determine if additional adjustments to compensate for the change must be made. Usually this involves a manual search through the code to identify any other affected modules. Depending on how many global variables or common modules are involved and how closely interrelated the modules are, the search may be difficult and time-consuming. In some instances, the search may require more effort than rewriting the code. Cross reference tables and execution flow maps can help in tracing the ripple effect of changes.

An objective in modifying software is to minimize the ripple effect. Not only will this simplify the task of implementing the change, but it may also lessen the risk of introducing errors as an unwanted side-effect of the change.

The following guidelines are suggested to help control the ripple effect arising from changes to software:

1. Change as little as possible.
2. Change as few variables as possible and, in particular, as few global variables as possible.
3. When a common module is changed, examine all modules that invoke this common module to determine if they are affected by the change. Also, examine all modules that are invoked by the common module to determine if they are affected by the change.
4. When a local variable (a *local variable* is referenced in only one module) is changed, examine the code in the module referencing the variable to determine if the function performed by this module or any other variables referenced in this module are affected by the change. Remember that a change to one variable may indirectly affect other variables if their value is determined in part by the changed variable.
5. When a global variable is changed or indirectly affected by a change, examine all modules referencing this global variable to determine the affect of the change on these modules.
6. When multiple changes must be performed to a software system, order the changes in the following manner:
    (i) Group changes by module.
    (ii) Plan the sequence of modules to be changed following the easiest first strategy; that is, make the easiest, smallest changes first.
    (iii) Change one module at a time.
    (iv) For each module changed, determine the ripple effect of the change before changing the next module in the sequence.
7. Use the ripple effect and complexity measures to determine the difficulty of making a change. For each change, C, the difficulty of making the change can be calculated by the following:

$$D(C) = \sum_{i=1}^{n} CM_i + \sum_{j=1}^{k} CM_j$$

Where CM_i is the complexity of each module m_i whose code must be modified to implement the change and where CM_j is the complexity of each module m_j whose code is indirectly affected by the change as a consequence of the ripple effect. For example, CM_i and CM_j may simply be calculated by counting the number of compares in module m_i and module m_j, respectively.
8. Before implementing a change, consider alternative implementation approaches. For each module directly affected by the change or indirectly affected due to the ripple effect, calculate its complexity before and after the change is implemented. Choose the change implementation approach that is the least difficult; that is, the approach that minimizes $D(C)$ and that does not increase program complexity.

6.3.6 Revalidating the Software

The final step of the maintenance process is to revalidate the software. We must demonstrate that the modifications are correctly implemented, that the software system as a whole still functions correctly, and that software quality has not been harmed by the modification.

The revalidation process resembles the development testing phase and consists of unit testing, integration testing, system testing, and acceptance testing steps (see Fig. 6.2). It is directed by the Software Complexity Profile and the Test History (see Tables 6.1 and 6.2). For example, as part of the revalidation unit testing step, each module changed is unit tested. In addition, those modules whose complexity has exceeded the guideline limits, or in which the errors discovered have exceeded the test history averages, are retested most thoroughly.

The following are guidelines for the revalidation process:

1. Revalidate the software using the unit test, integration test, system test, and acceptance test plans adapted from the software development testing phase.
2. Perform unit testing for each module modified. When possible use the unit tests and data from development testing and compare results to find any discrepancies.
3. Perform regression tests as each modified module is reintegrated into the software system, to determine if any other parts of the system have been adversely affected by the modification.
4. Referring to the Software Complexity Profile, execute integration, system, and acceptance tests that concentrate on the most complex parts of the software.
5. Perform system tests adapting the tests and data from development testing and compare results to find discrepancies.
6. Perform acceptance tests using the tests and data from development testing and also tests supplied by the user.
7. Use state-of-the-art test tools.
8. Create the Modification Test History by recording the information listed in Table 6.2.

Results of the revalidation testing are recorded in the Modification Test History so that comparisons can be made between these results and those obtained from development testing and previous revalidation efforts for the system. Comparison figures of particular interest are listed in Table 6.3. Increases in these figures over those from previous efforts may be the first indication of a decrease in software maintainability and, in general, in software quality.

Increases at the unit test level may indicate that the modifications were made too hastily or that the software documentation, technical tools, or programmer expertise used for the modification were inadequate. Increases at integration or system test level may indicate that unit testing was not thoroughly performed or that the ramification of the software modification was not well understood. An investigation of the errors may show that the errors discovered during revalidation were not introduced by modifications but were "left over"

Table 6.3. Measuring Changes in Maintainability.

Unit Test History

- Average Number of Errors Discovered per Module
- Total Number of Statements Modified to Correct Errors
- Average Length of Time to Discover and Correct an Error

Integration Test History

- Number of Errors Discovered
- Average Number of Errors Discovered per Module
- Number of Statements Modified to Correct Errors
- Number of Modules Modified to Correct Errors
- Average Length of Time to Discover and Correct an Error

System (Acceptance) Test History

- Number of Errors Discovered
- Average Number of Errors Discovered per Module
- Number of Statements Modified to Correct Errors
- Number of Modules Modified to Correct Errors
- Average Time to Discover and Correct an Error

from software development. In this case, the original quality of the software should be questioned. On the other hand, decreases in these figures may indicate a level of stability in software quality since fewer errors are being discovered.

Comparing revalidation errors with previous error statistics may help identify maintainability problem areas. This information can be used to suggest improvements in both the maintenance process and the development process and can be very beneficial in extending the software life. For example, modules that are error-prone based on the number of errors discovered during development testing and revalidation testing should be considered candidates for further complexity analysis and redesign. It is only by studying software as it is maintained that we can realistically evaluate its quality, the validity of our measures for software quality, and the effectiveness of our software development methods.

Revalidation also includes a check-point review for user and management acceptance of the modification. During this review, it is possible that the modification may be judged unacceptable, perhaps because of its effect on system usability or its error statistics. In such cases, the modification is not adopted and the software continues to be used in its original state until the modifications are made in a manner acceptable to the user and to management. We recommend the check-point review as a means of extending software life expectancy and as a management means for controlling the maintainer. We discuss the management aspects of the maintenance function in the next chapter.

6.4 SUMMARY

In this chapter, we studied the maintenance phase of the software life cycle. Maintenance is the function of keeping software operational. The difficulty of the maintenance function arises from problems such as:

- Poor quality of original software
- Inadequate documentation
- Limited test resources
- High learning curve due to the increasing complexity of new software systems

It also arises from the characteristic of most software to continually require change. The majority of changes are attributed to adapting to new processing and data requirements and to responding to user requests. A negative side effect of changing software is a deterioration of software quality leading to its eventual obsolescence. As a means of combatting these maintenance problems, we structured maintenance into a multi-step process directed by the software engineering discipline used in software development efforts.

The maintenance process consists of four basic steps:

1. Understand the software.
2. Determine what to modify.
3. Implement the modification.
4. Revalidate the software.

Understanding a software system is the first step in maintaining it. To reduce the learning curve, the software maintainer should participate in the software development process. The maintainer should develop maintainability acceptance criteria that are enforced during each development phase check-point review. Also, during the software development process, the maintainer should develop a Maintenance Support Plan identifying requirements for maintaining the software.

The process of determining requirements and methods in modifying software parallels the process of determining needs and capabilities in developing it. We divide this maintenance step into three phases:

1. Requirements Analysis
2. Specification
3. Design

Besides defining a correct, efficient modification approach, our objective is to limit the effect of the modification on other parts of the software and on user interfaces. At the completion of this step, a check-point review is included as a means of preserving software quality and of assessing the value of the modification.

During the third step of the maintenance process, we modify the software code. Our objective is to correctly and efficiently translate the design for the modification into well-structured code. Our approach is:

- To change as little as possible
- To evaluate the changes in terms of complexity and ripple effect
- To document the changes and the change process
- To require a code inspection by someone other than the maintenance programmer who coded the changes

During the final step of the maintenance process, we demonstrate that the modification to the specifications have been correctly implemented, that the software system as a whole still functions correctly, and that the software quality has not been degraded. Revalidation parallels the software development testing phase and includes unit testing, integration testing, system testing, and acceptance testing. Test cases and data from development testing are adapted for use in revalidation testing and results from development tests and previous revalidation tests are compared to reveal any discrepancies. Also, errors are compared as a means of determining if software quality has been degraded by the maintenance process. Revalidation includes a check-point review to determine if the modification should be accepted for inclusion in the installed version of the software.

7
Controlling Software Maintenance

7.1 INTRODUCTION

Management of the software maintenance function is out of control. Although a majority of the systems and programming effort in many organizations is spent on maintenance, management has little information on what activities comprise the maintenance function, who is responsible for which software application systems, and what is the source of most maintenance work. According to a recent survey, most maintenance performed falls into the category of perfective maintenance—maintenance performed to improve software maintainability, to enhance software performance, or to accommodate user requests.[1] Without adequate information, it is difficult for management to evaluate the legitimacy of this type of maintenance with respect to software life cycle goals and overall organization goals, or to evaluate the necessity of devoting the majority of its software staff to maintenance. This is an extremely serious management problem because it directly affects an organization's ability to meet future software system demands. If management controls are not applied, the maintenance function may absorb all systems and programming resources, leaving nothing for the development of new software systems.

The problem of controlling the maintenance function raises several questions:

1. Are most user requests based upon well-thought-out, legitimate requirements or personal preferences?
2. Could software changes be performed more efficiently if user requests were better controlled and maintenance personnel better trained?

3. Are maintenance programmers performing perfective maintenance because of their propensity for tuning or because performance improvements can be justified in terms of user benefits and cost savings?
4. What portion of the maintenance problem can be attributed to poorly defined user requirements, poorly defined functional specifications, or poorly implemented and tested code?

The first step in controlling the maintenance function is to understand what is being done and why. We need to apply to software maintenance activities the formal controls used in software development projects. We need to:

- Categorize and record maintenance tasks.
- Organize the maintenance staff to better identify individual responsibilities.
- Control user requests with formalized change control procedures and an open communication channel between the maintenance group and user groups.
- Give feedback to the software developer on how well the system works and meets user needs in practice.

In this chapter, we address the problem of poor management control of the maintenance function by defining an organizational structure for the maintenance staff and a change request procedure.

7.2 MAINTENANCE TEAMS

7.2.1 Maintenance Organization Requirements

In Chapter 4, we discussed organizational structures for software development project teams. Our objective was to make the software development process more visible to management and more amenable to management controls. In this chapter, our objective for the maintenance process is the same—to make the maintenance process more visible to management and more amenable to management controls.

The lack of a formal organizational structure in many maintenance staffs has contributed to problems of identifying individual responsibilities, of providing adequate motivation, of preserving software quality, of making appropriate, timely support decisions, and of providing open communication channels within the maintenance group and with outside groups. We need an organizational structure for the maintenance staff that can accomplish the following:

- Enhance software visibility so that the software can be subjected to periodic quality control audit reviews.
- Formalize the maintenance organization so that individual responsibilities and assignments are clearly defined.
- Establish communication channels between the maintenance staff and the outside organization including management, user groups, and the software development staff.
- Encourage an open, egoless maintenance environment in which state-of-the-art tools can be mastered and applied.
- Avoid software support dependency on one individual staff member.

The programming team structure is well-suited to meet these needs. The maintenance team structure presented in this chapter is adopted from the software development team structures presented in Chapter 4.

7.2.2 Maintenance Team Structure

The maintenance staff is organized into teams of two or more members. A minimum team size of two is necessary to avoid the vulnerable management situation of depending upon one particular individual for support of a software system. Each team is assigned software support responsibilities for a specified group of software programs. This identifies who is responsible for which software programs, allowing management to direct requests and questions to the appropriate team.

A team is assembled for the duration of the life cycle of the software programs it supports. Although individual membership in the team may change, the team itself continues to exist as long as it has software to maintain. This provides continuity of support throughout the final life cycle phase.

Maintenance support responsibilities begin at the completion of the development phases when the software becomes a production system,

166 PART 3 MANAGING SOFTWARE MAINTENANCE

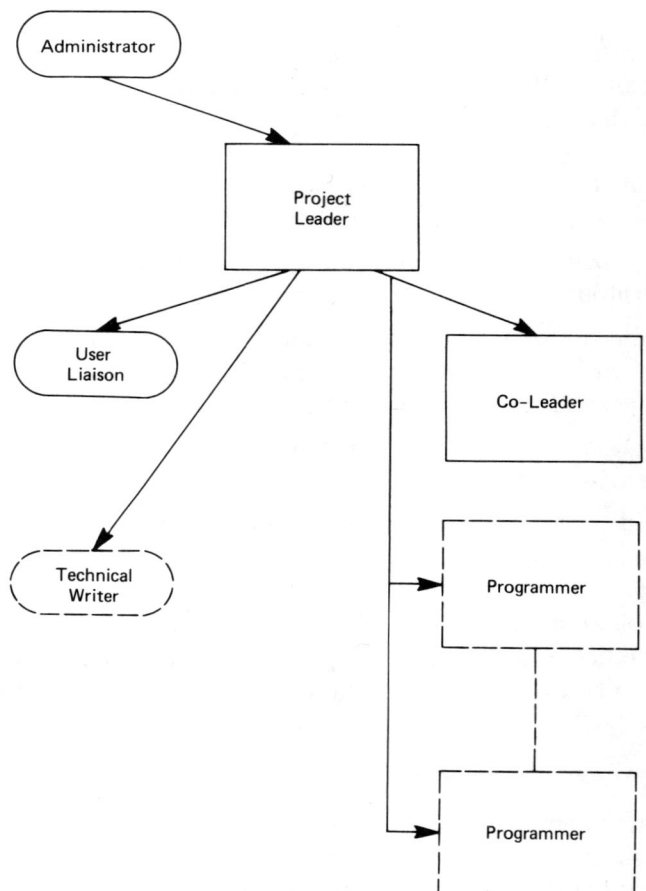

Fig. 7.1. Revised chief programmer team structure.

and include all maintenance functions such as error detection and correction, adaptation to data and processing environment changes, and responses to user requests. However, support preparations begin during the software development or package selection phases.

Team organization is patterned after the Revised Chief Programmer Team (RCPT) structure presented in Chapter 4 (see Fig. 7.1). Like the software development team, the maintenance team requires the discipline, specialization of function, and open, egoless work environment that is offered by the RCPT structure.

Recall from Chapter 4 that the nucleus of the RCPT structure consists of a project leader, a co-leader, a user liaison, and a project administrator. The project leader is the technical leader of the team and is responsible for software product development. He reports to the project administrator, and all other team members report to him. The co-leader is the technical assistant of the project leader. He is groomed to assume the team leadership role in the event that the project leader leaves the team. Also, he serves as the team technical liaison representing the team in technical meetings with outside groups and providing a communication link to the maintenance group during software development. The user liaison provides the communication link between the development team and the user group. The project administrator is the administrative head of the team and performs the interface function with upper management.

The base RCPT structure can be expanded to include a group of programmers responsible for coding and testing the software under the direction of the project leader.

The maintenance adaptation of the RCPT structure consists of a maintenance leader, a co-leader, a user liaison, a maintenance administrator and, optionally, a group of maintenance programmers.

The *maintenance leader* is directly responsible for the technical support of a set of software programs. He reports to the maintenance administrator, and the rest of the maintenance team reports to him. The maintenance leader is an experienced systems analyst, is trained in project management, and is knowledgeable in the application areas of the software supported.

The *co-leader* of the maintenance team is the assistant to the maintenance leader. He is qualified to assume team leadership in the event that the maintenance leader leaves the team. Like the maintenance leader, he is an experienced systems analyst, a trained project leader, and is knowledgeable in the software application areas. He performs the liaison function with the development staff of the systems and programming department and with other teams. He is responsible for tracking the development of a new software system slated to be supported by his team. During the development phases, he attends each introduction and checkpoint review, he defines software maintainability acceptance criteria, he audits the software for compliance to these criteria, and gathers information needed for maintenance support preparations.

During the maintenance phase, the co-leader continues to interact with the software developers. He reports feedback on the software's behavior as a production system. For example, he reports error frequency rates, problems with software quality, actual changes compared to changes predicted by the developers, and so forth. This type of feedback is critical for software developers since it can confirm or raise serious doubts about the value of various software engineering tools and techniques employed and the resulting software quality.

Since a large portion of maintenance work is generated by user requests, the *user liaison* function is as important in the maintenance phase as in the development phases. The user liaison is a specialist in the application area and is responsible for communications between the user groups and the software maintenance team. The user liaison serves as a buffer protecting the maintenance team from direct and continual user interruptions.

The *maintenance administrator* function is performed by the supervisor of the maintenance staff. He is the administrative head of the maintenance team with hiring, firing, and promotion responsibility for all members of the team. He provides the communication link with management. Usually, one maintenance administrator has charge of several maintenance teams.

The *maintenance programmers* are responsible for diagnosing software problems and implementing modifications to the software under the direction of the maintenance leader. They are assigned tasks on the basis of their individual skills and experiences. Not all maintenance programmers should be programmer trainees since many maintenance assignments involve difficult and critical programming tasks. Allowing inexperienced programmers to modify complex software systems without experienced supervision has caused software quality degradation and has hastened the obsolescence of many software systems.

Before assigning maintenance tasks to team members, the maintenance leader should review the Systems Development Journal. Information such as the original development philosophy should be explained to the maintenance team in an effort to preserve system integrity as it was defined by the original software development team. Also, the maintenance leader should review the Complexity Profile, the Test History, and development problems cited in the System

Development Journal to identify the most complex parts of the system. Maintenance assignments requiring analysis and/or modification to these parts of the system should be given to the more experienced team members. When this is not possible, the maintenance leader should carefully oversee the performance of these tasks.

Assigning very difficult tasks to inexperienced personnel or assigning very straightforward tasks to experienced personnel may result in increasing program complexity. In the case of an inexperienced programmer, additional complexity may be introduced because the ripple effect of the modification is not properly evaluated. In the case of an experienced programmer, additional complexity may be introduced as a consequence of attempting to make the software, and likewise the assignment, more interesting.

Not only program complexity, but also programmer productivity is affected by the choice of personnel assigned to a particular task. Normally, the more experienced the programmer, the more quickly the task can be accomplished. In some cases, if the task is beyond the experience level of the programmer, it will never be completed. However, the assignment of very simple tasks to experienced personnel also runs the risk of never being completed. In this case, the experienced programmer may set aside simpler tasks in favor of working on more challenging problems. For example, in the SMCS project discussed in Chapter 2, we saw that the programmers achieved a lower productivity rate on the simpler tasks than on the more difficult tasks because they found the simpler tasks boring.

Technical training for maintenance programmers should be similar to that provided for development programmers. Also, specialization should be encouraged. Besides developing toolsmith, language lawyer, or tester skills,[2] the maintenance programmer should be encouraged to develop skills in the areas of performance tuning and error analysis and an indepth knowledge of the application areas.

7.2.3 A Solution to Maintenance Problems

Organizing the maintenance staff into maintenance teams (see Fig. 7.2) as we described above is a means of addressing several frequently cited maintenance problems such as:[3]

170 PART 3 MANAGING SOFTWARE MAINTENANCE

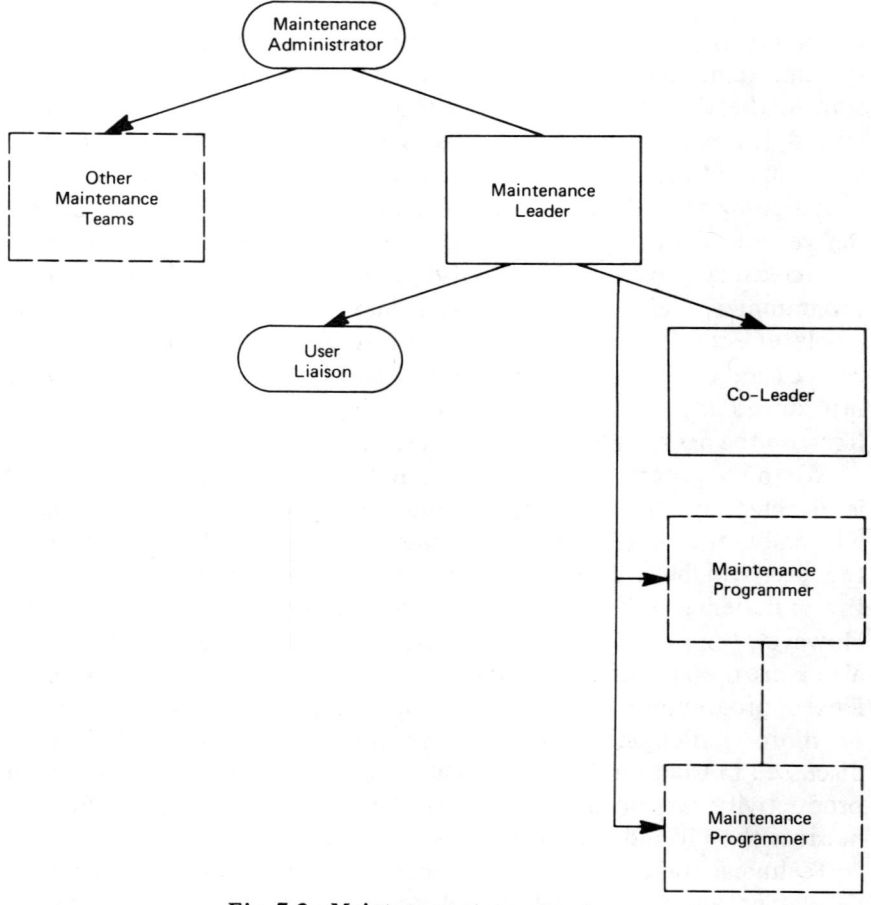

Fig. 7.2. Maintenance team structure.

- User demands for enhancements
- Quality of the original software
- Quality of the maintenance personnel
- High learning curve due to the size of the software system

First, the maintenance staff can be protected from a continual barrage of user demands by funnelling user requests through the user liaison. This provides management with a mechanism for controlling change requests as well as identifying long-term user needs. We discuss this further in the next section.

Second, assigning development personnel to the maintenance area can reduce the learning curve for large systems and improve the quality of maintenance personnel. Also, forcing software developers to maintain software reinforces the necessity of developing high quality software.

Third, using a similar team structure in both the development area and the maintenance area allows easier exchange of personnel in both directions. Not only should development personnel be assigned to the maintenance area, but also maintenance personnel should be assigned to the development area. Rotating software personnel between the two groups will create greater flexibility in staffing, improve overall personnel experience level, create a sense of appreciation for the technical expertise required in both areas, and lessen the stigma attached to performing maintenance tasks.

7.2.4 Maintenance Team Staffing

The effort required to support a software system varies over time and with changes to the system.[4] Because of scheduling constraints and unforseen development problems, software systems often are not entirely completed during the development portion of the life cycle. The implementation of less critical system functions, final documentation drafts, and performance tuning are often postponed until the maintenance phase. A more modest version of the software is temporarily released to the user while enhancements are performed to upgrade the software to its intended capabilities level. This along with correcting errors not discovered during development causes the maintenance effort for a newly released software system to be initially high and then decrease until the next major release of the software occurs, and then this cycle is repeated (see Fig. 7.3).

To provide for the greater maintenance support needs of a newly released software system some members of the original software development should be recruited as members of the maintenance team (see Fig. 7.4). This may be considered a temporary assignment until all software development work has been completed and the system

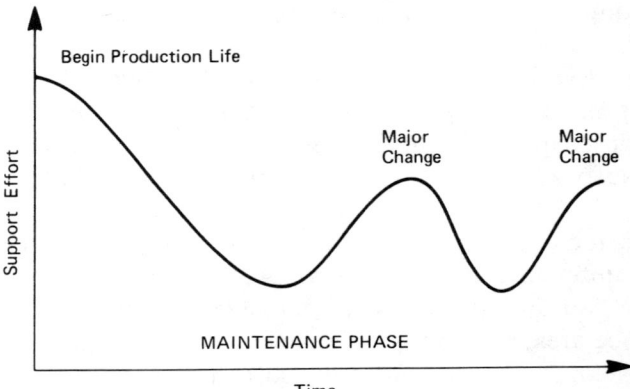

Fig. 7.3. Software maintenance effort over time.

behavior appears stablized in terms of reliability, efficiency, and maintainability requirements.

An ideal candidate for the maintenance leader is the co-leader of the original software development team. Having provided the communication link to the maintenance group during the development phases and being intimately familiar with the software, the co-leader is in an excellent position to direct maintenance activities, especially when the software is first released for use as a production system.

To provide continuity in communications with the user group, the person who performed the user liaison function is the ideal candidate to fill the user liaison position in the maintenance team. In large systems, the user liaison function is probably performed by a group rather than one individual. It is advantageous in this case that at least one member of the original user liaison group continue to perform the user liaison function during the maintenance phase.

Including some members of the original software development team in the maintenance team is beneficial for several reasons. First, while working with members of the original development team, other members of the maintenance team can learn firsthand about the development philosophy and the developer's approach for ensuring software quality and system integrity. Also, they can learn how to use state-of-the-art software development techniques and tools. On the other hand, members of the development team can observe firsthand how well the software performs in practice. Second, borrowing develop-

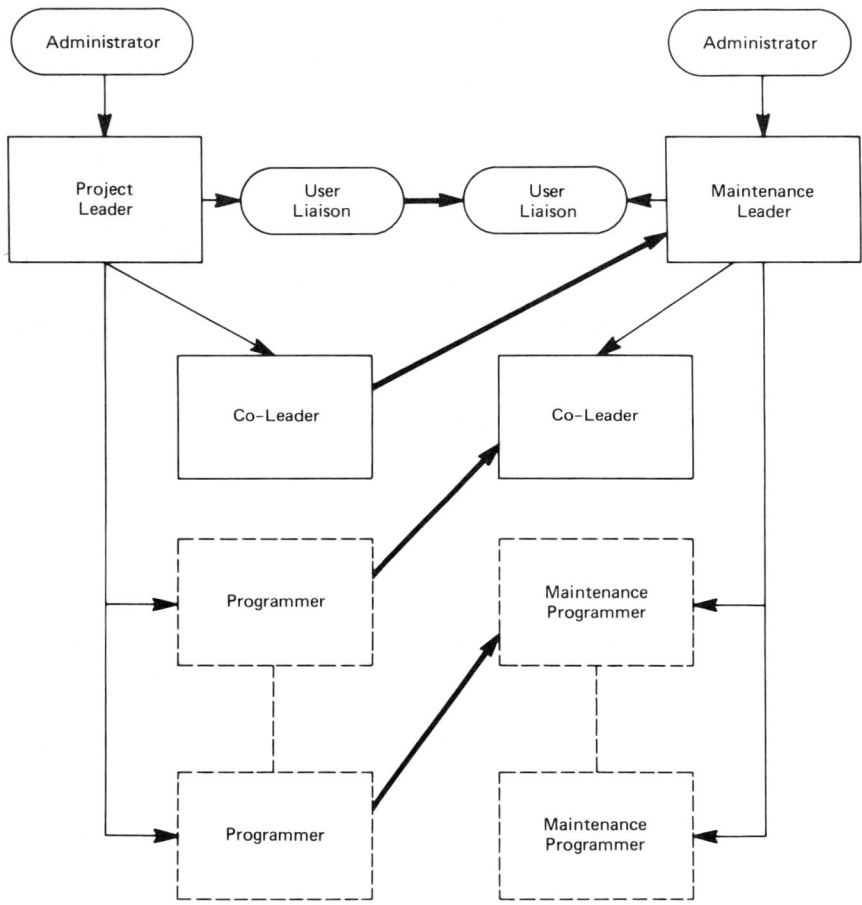

Fig. 7.4. Recruiting software development personnel for the maintenance team.

ment personnel to supplement the maintenance staff during the initial system release period can help avoid temporary software staffing shortages.

Third, rotating development programmers into the maintenance area will help break down the barrier between the two programming factions. In many systems and programming groups, the programming personnel in the development group are entirely separate from the programming personnel in the maintenance group. The development group is considered an elitist group since only trainees and programmers who cannot keep up with technological advances are typically relegated to the maintenance group. Also, the more challenging tasks, experience with state-of-the-art tools, and better promotion possibilities are given to the development group. This practice has created an unhealthy competition between the two groups which has adversely affected their ability to support software.

We found in the last chapter that the maintenance of a software system is a very challenging, difficult task. We also found that relegating this task to junior level software personnel has caused many maintenance problems leading to total software system degradation. Including development personnel in the software maintenance staff is one means of improving the experience level in the maintenance group and, in general, of improving software support.

7.3 CONTROLLING SOFTWARE CHANGES

7.3.1 A Management Problem

The outstanding management problem for the software maintenance organization is controlling changes made to software systems. In the last chapter, we learned that software is continually changed to correct software failures, to adapt to processing environment changes, and to accommodate user requests. We also learned that a large percentage of changes are made to accommodate user requests.[5]

Managing changes in an effective and economical manner requires an understanding of why a change is needed, of the effort required to make the change, and of the effect of implementing the change in terms of software quality and user satisfaction. As a first step in managing software change, change information must be recorded. This information is useful in making a determination to approve or reject a change request, in planning for long term maintenance efforts required to support a software system, and in studying the ability of a software design to accommodate changes.

As a second step, a change control procedure must be used to aid management in monitoring changes. It also ensures that change requests will be handled in a professional manner. Each individual requesting a change should be notified of the status of the request in a timely fashion regardless of whether the change request is accepted, rejected, or temporarily tabled.

7.3.2 Justifying a Software Change

Requests for software change come from the user community, from the software development group, from the maintenance group, from the operations group, and from management. These requests, depending upon the reason given for the change, can be classified into the three maintenance categories:[6]

1. Corrective changes
2. Adaptive changes
3. Perfective changes

Regardless of the requester or the change category, no request should result in a software modification without careful consideration. Even a simple change can have subtle, yet very serious ramifications on the life of a software system. Also, many changes cannot be justified in terms of increased usability or performance improvements. For example, users often tend to exaggerate their needs for a particular enhancement, and then after the enhancement is implemented, it is seldom used.[7] Finally, change requests should be considered in the context of other change requests and how they relate to the system life cycle plan. For example, a similar request may have been submitted by several different requesters. On the other hand, different requesters may suggest changes that are incompatible with each other or incompatible with life cycle goals.

When considering a change, questions such as the following should be addressed:[8]

1. Is the maintenance objective to preserve a single version of the software system for all user groups or to allow different versions to support different user groups?
2. Is this a temporary software system slated to be replaced in the near future?
3. Will this change alter the original scope and purpose of the software?

Each time a software system is changed, there is a risk of introducing additional errors into the software and of jeopardizing software quality.[9] Although this risk can be reduced by building reliable, modifiable software, it is always present to some degree because of the complex nature of software. Therefore, our basic operating premise for managing software change is that we do *not* change software unless the change can be justified in terms of a set of meaningful, explicit criteria.

The justification for corrective changes is straightforward. Usually, the change will be implemented on the justification that the software must function correctly. In some cases, however, the cost or the effect on the rest of the software may be so great compared to the minor inconvenience resulting from the software failure that the user may choose to tolerate the failure rather than risk introducing new problems as an unwanted side-effect of the change.

The justification for adaptive changes and perfective changes may be more complicated since the benefits compared to the cost of implementing and the risk of degrading software quality may be difficult to evaluate.

The specific justification criteria depend upon the needs and priorities of a particular organization, but generally should include:

- Total cost of the change
- Manpower requirements to implement the change
- Elapsed time needed to implement the change
- Disruption to current service
- Retraining needed for operation personnel and user groups
- Effect on software quality
- Compatibility with software life cycle plan
- Ramifications on future changes to the software
- Risk of reducing software life expectancy

Emphasis should be placed on those criteria measuring the long-term effect on software life expectancy rather than on the ability of a change to satisfy the user or to improve performance for the short term with an apparently low-cost modification. Decisions to change software that are based on a response to user pressure, or that rely upon the maintenance programmer's personal scheme for performance tuning, have helped create patchwork software that soon becomes a maintenance nightmare.

7.3.3 Change Request Procedure

The excuse that maintenance tasks cannot be planned since it is impossible to predict when a critical failure requiring immediate attention may occur applies only to a small percentage of all maintenance tasks. The majority of the maintenance effort arises in response to change requests that can be controlled and planned.

An essential management tool for controlling software change is a formal change request procedure whose purposes are:

- To record each change request for the purpose of studying how software changes and planning for support needs
- To provide a followup procedure for every request with a report to the requester of the planned software change or the reason for rejecting the request
- To ensure that changes are planned and scheduled allowing maintenance tasks to be planned and scheduled

A change request procedure is summarized in Fig. 7.5. This is an outline of a general procedure to serve as a guideline in developing a change request procedure for a particular maintenance organization. For some organizations, it may be too detailed, for others not detailed enough. The key point is that every maintenance organization requires some type of formal change request procedure to control the change requests and to serve the user in an expedient manner.

The steps of a general change request procedure are defined in detail in the remainder of this section.

Step 1. In the initial step of the change request procedure, the requester fills out a change request form and submits it to the maintenance group for consideration. The change request form (see Table 7.1) contains information such as the requester's name, the date of the request, the type of change requested, the software system to be changed, the reason for making the request, and the urgency of the change. Requests for repairs to software failures as well as software enhancements may be reported on the change request form.

Table 7.1. Change Request.

```
                          Table 7.1
                        Change Request


Requester: _____ Date: _____
Application _____ Program: _____


Type of Change

   _____ Corrective

   _____ Adaptive

   _____ Perfective


Reason for Requesting Change
_____
_____
_____


Date Change Needed: _____


Priority Number

   _____ 0 Tabled

   _____ 1 Critical

   _____ 2 Important

   _____ 3 Optional


Approvals
User Liaison _____ Date: _____
Recommendation _____
_____

Maintenance Leader _____ Date: _____
Recommendation _____
_____
```

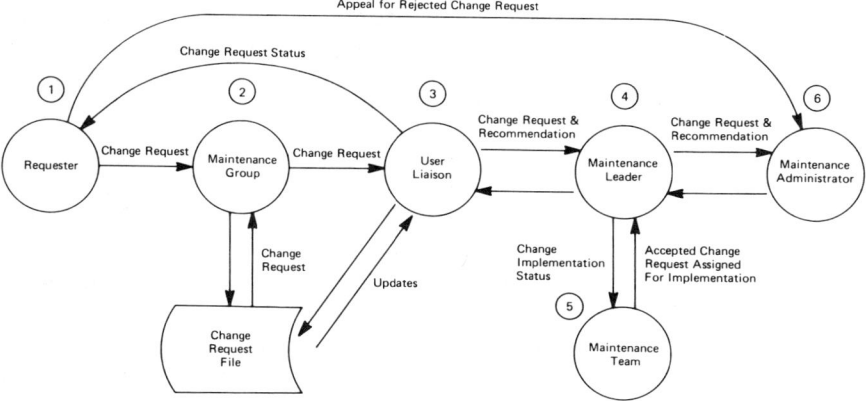

Fig. 7.5. Change request procedure.

Step 2. Upon receipt of the change request into the maintenance group, the request is entered into the change request file and assigned a change request number. The change request file should be part of an automated maintenance journal. It contains status information on all active change requests under consideration or under implementation in the maintenance area.

Step 3. The change request is given to the user liaison who is responsible for the support of the affected software system. In some cases, it is possible that a change request may affect more than one software system. In these cases, all appropriate user liaisons should evaluate the request.

The user liaison notifies the requester that the request is under investigation. To alleviate the frustration that users often experience with poor response to their needs, it is very important to keep the user informed of the status of each request.

The user liaison conducts a preliminary study to determine the effort needed to make the change, the justification for the change, its feasibility, its cost, and so forth. During the study, the user liaison may interview the requester, the maintenance group, and the system developer. The purpose of the study is to gather enough information upon which to make an initial recommendation to accept, reject, or table the request. The recommendation should be based upon the set of explicit criteria defined for the maintenance organization (see Section 7.3.2). As part of the recommendation, the user liaison assigns a priority number to the request:

- 0 *Tabled*—Should be reconsidered for a later release.
- 1 *Critical*—Should receive immediate attention ahead of currently scheduled maintenance tasks.
- 2 *Important*—Should be placed at the end of the list of tasks that must be performed for this release.
- 3 *Optional*—Should be placed at the end of the list of tasks that, time and resources permitting, should be performed for this release.

Step 4. The user liaison submits the change request accompanied by his recommendation to his maintenance leader for consideration. Change requests assigned a critical priority number (1) should be submitted immediately. Less critical change requests may be submitted at the team status meeting.

The maintenance leader may override the priority number assigned or the recommendation made by the user liaison, or may request that a more comprehensive study be performed by the user liaison and the maintenance co-leader before a decision is made regarding the request.

Change requests that are accepted by the maintenance leader and that require a minor effort to implement (with "minor" defined as one man-month or less) may be scheduled as a maintenance task by the maintenance leader. Change requests that are accepted by the maintenance leader but require more than a minor effort to complete or alter the software life cycle plan are considered major changes and must be reviewed by the maintenance administrator. Critical changes should be submitted for review immediately; other change requests should be submitted at the maintenance administrator status meeting.

The user liaison reports the status of the change request to the requester at the end of this step. The user liaison also records the proposed implementation schedule for accepted change requests, and the reject recommendation for rejected change requests, in the change request file.

Step 5. Accepted requests are scheduled for implementation and assigned to the maintenance team by the maintenance leader. The user liaison informs the requester that the request has been scheduled.

When the change is completed, the user liaison informs the requester and updates the change request file accordingly.

Step 6. Change requests that require a major effort or alter the life cycle plan (e.g., require that multiple current versions of the software be supported when the maintenance plan included only one current version) must be approved by the maintenance administrator. Since the ramifications from such changes on software life expectancy and long term support may be very severe, such change requests must be carefully considered in terms of long-range goals for the maintenance organization as well as in terms of short-range costs and effort.

The maintenance administrator may override the maintenance leader's recommendation and the priority number assigned to the request.

If the maintenance administrator accepts the change request, its implementation becomes the responsibility of the maintenance leader.

Requests that were previously rejected may be appealed by the requester to the maintenance administrator.

The user liaison informs the requester of the status of the change request and updates the change request file at the end of this step.

7.4 SUMMARY

In this chapter, we discussed the need for management control of the maintenance function. We presented two mechanisms for achieving better management control:

1. An organizational structure for the management staff
2. A change request procedure

We suggested organizing the maintenance staff into maintenance teams whose structure closely resembles the Revised Chief Programmer Team structure used for software development project teams. The nucleus of the maintenance team consists of a maintenance leader, a co-leader, a user liaison, and a maintenance administrator. Optionally, the maintenance team may include a group of maintenance programmers. One maintenance team may be responsible for the support of several software systems.

There were several benefits cited for organizing the maintenance staff into teams. First, explicitly defining individual responsibilities enables management to monitor task progress and to assess individual contributions. Second, using an organizational structure similar to that used for software development teams allows easier exchange of technical personnel between the two groups for increased staffing flexibility and increased sharing of experienced personnel. Third, establishing an explicit communication link via the user liaison between the maintenance group and user groups provides improved user support.

We suggested a formal change request procedure as a means of handling the continual stream of user requests barraging the maintenance group. The purposes of the procedure are:

1. To improve management's ability to plan for and to schedule software changes
2. To ensure that change requests are recorded
3. To ensure that change requests are accepted only if they can be justified by a set of explicit, meaningful criteria
4. To ensure that the requester is informed of the status of a request in a timely manner

The change request procedure is designed to expedite the response to change requests but not at the expense of carefully evaluating the benefits and the risks of accommodating the request. Emphasis is placed on long-term ramifications to software quality rather than on short-term user satisfaction. Although this approach will not always answer a request with the expected software change, it will greatly improve software service for the user and will help control rising software maintenance costs.

Part 4
Conclusion

8
Evaluating the Software Life Cycle

8.1 STUDYING SOFTWARE PROJECTS

Because most software projects fall behind schedule and because management is anxious to begin the next software project from a continually growing backlog of user requests, we, as software engineers, have not taken the time to look back. We seldom review what we have done to learn from past successes and failures. The pressure to meet growing demands for more software and to remain state-of-the-art has overshadowed the importance of evaluating how well software performs as a user tool and how well software engineering principles work in practice.

Although we have made great strides in the past decade, we have a great deal more to learn about producing and supporting well-engineered, useful software. The current state-of-the-art is plagued with failures. Management is bewildered by its inability to control the information processing function. Users are frustrated and antagonized by the introduction of software systems that are difficult to use and that do not work as expected. Software engineers are at a loss to understand why one project succeeds and the next one fails.

Recording and studying software project case histories must become a required, not optional, component of every software project. We must recognize software engineering as an applied, not a theoretical, discipline. Defining software engineering principles and methodologies is only the first step. We also must evaluate their utility in practice. A major problem blocking software improvements is the lack of reported software project case histories. It is difficult to convince management of the value of trying new methodologies when there is no supporting evidence to draw upon. Also, it is difficult to speculate where further research is needed.

In Chapter 2, we presented two project case histories to illustrate the value of studying past software efforts. Studying how well our principles and methodologies work in practice may be the best method of improving software and the software life cycle process.

This is not a new philosophy. It has often been advocated in software engineering literature. For example, the final principle listed in Boehm's seven basic principles of software engineering is:

Maintain a commitment to improve the process.[1]

Boehm explains that fundamental to the process of producing quality software is a commitment on the part of the software developer to continually seek ways in which to improve the software product and its production. New software engineering techniques and tools should be tried in actual projects. Methods to evaluate the effect of these tools should be defined. Data should be collected and analyzed to determine production bottlenecks, poor schedule and cost estimates, and error frequencies.

Although advocated, this principle is seldom practiced. To emphasize the importance of its application in practice we add an evaluation phase to the software life cycle (see Fig. 8.1).

Throughout this book we have stressed the importance of defining the software qualities and the project priorities sought in a software activity. Also, we have stressed the importance of establishing a communication channel between the software developer, upper management, the user, and the software maintainer. Finally, we have stressed the importance of recording each phase of the software life cycle. One purpose is to establish an environment and to provide information that can be used in evaluating software engineering and software products.

We are interested in two types of evaluation:

1. Evaluation of a software product
2. Evaluation of the software life cycle process

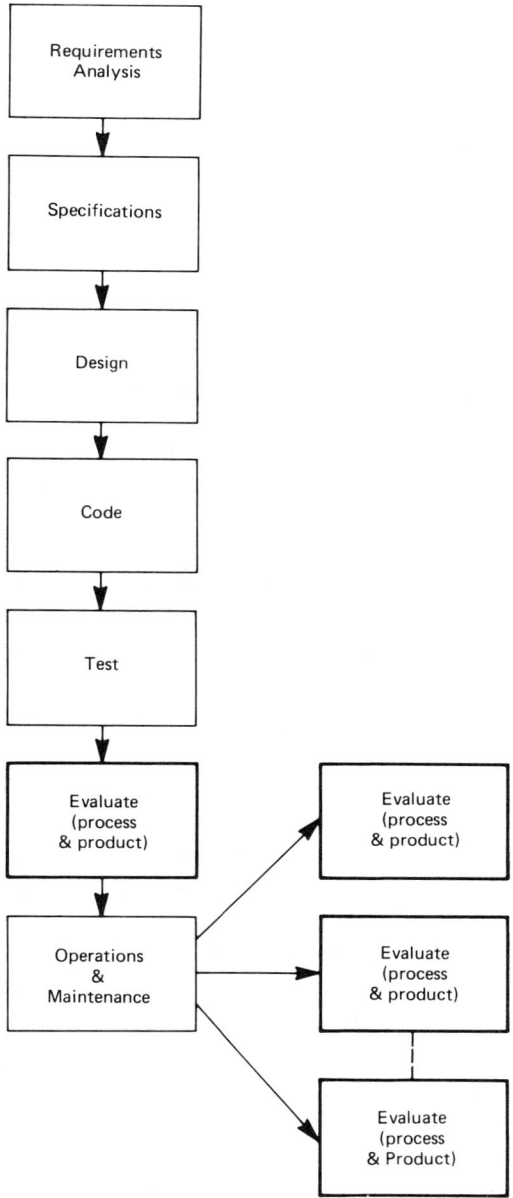

Fig. 8.1. Software life cycle evaluation phase.

8.2 EVALUATING A SOFTWARE PRODUCT

The first evaluation of a software product is performed at the completion of the software development project. The software product is evaluated from several viewpoints:

1. User
2. Developer
3. Maintainer
4. Management

Each viewpoint has its own set of evaluation criteria. For example, the user evaluates software in terms of its usefulness. Does the software do the job intended? How easy is it to use? How available is it? Was it ready on schedule? Did it exceed anticipated costs to develop or to use?

The developer evaluates the software product more in terms of its structure than its usability. Is it reliable? Is it well-structured? Is it efficient?

The maintainer evaluates it primarily in terms of the quality of maintainability. Is it reliable? Is it easy to understand and to change? Is the documentation adequate? Is the code readable?

Management evaluates it in terms of how well it performs its intended function within cost and resource constraints. Is the opportunity loss and the risk to develop offset by the return on investment?

The evaluation is the responsibility of the software development team. It is considered a required postdevelopment/preproduction step that must be performed before a software product can be accepted into the operation and maintenance phase of its life cycle. It is based upon measures and standards for software quality that were established at the beginning of the software life cycle. The purpose of the study is to evaluate how well the software meets established quality criteria and organization standards.

Based upon information obtained from the user, the development team, the system maintainer, and upper management, an evaluation report is assembled by the project leader. Information is obtained by using the various communication links defined for the team (see Chapter 4, Section 4.3). For example, the user liaison interviews the user group to compile the user's evaluation of the software, the co-leader interviews the system maintainer, and the project administrator interviews upper management.

The evaluation report is a valuable software development tool for several reasons. First, it gives the development team feedback on the initial perception of software quality. This feedback will help reinforce the notion that the quality of software does not lie entirely in its form, but also lies in its utility, maintainability, and so forth. Second, it is useful to the developer in planning for future software development efforts. It may point out shortcomings in this software product that can be avoided in future software products. Third, it can be used as a learning tool to help software engineers better understand what makes a "good" software product.

The evaluation report should be included with other software documents as part of the permanent history of the software.

In addition to evaluating software when it enters the operation and maintenance phase, it also should be evaluated periodically during its final life cycle phase. As we pointed out in Part III, software quality often deteriorates during the maintenance phase. Periodic examination of software quality may help extend the useful life of software products.

This type of evaluation is the responsibility of the system maintainer.

8.3 EVALUATING THE SOFTWARE LIFE CYCLE PROCESS

We divide evaluation of the software process into two types:

1. Evaluation of the software development process
2. Evaluation of the software maintenance process

Evaluation of the software development process is performed by the project leader at the completion of the testing phase. Its purpose is to evaluate the software engineering techniques and tools used during development.

In Part II, we suggested that the project leader record the development process in the System Development Journal. Recall that the System Development Journal contains information such as system philosophy, development approach, decision-making strategy, project goals and priorities, experimental techniques and tools used, day-to-day problems experienced, and project successes and failures. Control documents such as status reports, estimated and actual incident reports, and change reports are also recorded as part of the project history.

At the beginning of the project, goals, priorities, standards, and procedures were defined by management. These, along with the Guidelines for Software Development presented in Chapter 1, are used as criteria against which to evaluate the software development process.

When examining the project history, the project leader should attempt to answer several questions. Did the project meet the goals and priorities established by management and those established by the project team? What new techniques and tools were tried? What was their effect on the project? Where were the bottlenecks? What were the major problems encountered? Where were there losses of management control in the project? In general, what was done "right" and what was done "wrong"? What was the attitude of members of the development team toward the project and the software they developed?

The project leader should evaluate the project immediately upon completion and should share his findings with this team, with other project teams, with management, and with the software engineering community at large.

Although Boehm's principles of software engineering emphasize the need to evaluate the software development process, it is just as important to evaluate the maintenance process. This is especially true now that the maintenance process absorbs most of our programming resources.

The maintenance process should be evaluated periodically by the maintenance leader. Evaluation documents include the System Maintenance Journal, the Test/Revalidation History, and the Guidelines for Software Maintenance. The leader's findings should be shared with the maintenance team to improve maintenance support, and with development teams to improve the overall software life cycle process.

Chapter Notes

Chapter 1

1. A. Wasserman, "Panel on Problems of the 80's," in the *3rd International Conference on Software Engineering Proc.* (Atlanta), May 10-12, 1978, p. 341.
2. B. Boehm, "Seven Basic Principles of Software Engineering," in *Infotech State of the Art Reports: Software Engineering Techniques* (Maidenhead, England: Infotech International, 1977): 77-113.
3. B. DeRoze and T. Nyman, "The Software Life Cycle–A Management and Technological Challenge in the Department of Defense," *IEEE Trans. on Soft. Eng.* SE-4, no. 4 (July 1978): 309-318.
4. P. Wegner, "Research Directions in Software Technology," in the *3rd International Conference on Software Engineering Proc.* (Atlanta), May 10-12, 1978, pp. 243-259.
5. B. Boehm, "Software and Its Impact: A Quantitative Assessment," *Datamation* 19, no. 5 (May 1973): 48-59.
6. M. Zelkowitz, "Perspectives on Software Engineering," *Computing Surveys* 10, no. 2 (June 1978): 297-316.
7. C. Liu, "A Look at Software Maintenance," *Datamation* 22, no. 11 (November 1976): 51-55.
8. DeRoze and Nyman, "The Software Life Cycle," pp. 309-318.
9. B. Lientz, E. Swanson and G. Tompkins, "Characteristics of Application Software Maintenance," *CACM* 21, no. 6 (June 1978): 466-471.
10. DeRoze and Nyman, "The Software Life Cycle," pp. 309-318.
11. B. Boehm, "Seven Basic Principles of Software Engineering," pp. 77-113.

Chapter 2

1. B. Boehm, "Seven Basic Principles of Software Engineering," in the *Infotech State of the Art Reports: Software Engineering Techniques* (Maidenhead, England: Infotech International, 1977): 77-113.
2. F. Baker and H. Mills, "Chief Programmer Teams," *IBM Systems Journal* 11, no. 1 (1972): 56-73.

3. C. McClure, *Reducing COBOL Complexity through Structured Programming*, (New York, New York: Van Nostrand Reinhold, 1978): 123-154.
4. C. McClure, *Reducing COBOL Complexity*, pp. 31-42.

Chapter 3

1. B. Knight, "On Software Quality and Productivity," in *Technical Directions*, IBM Federal Systems Division, July, 1978, pp. 21-27.
2. H. Mills, "Software Development," *IEEE Trans. on Soft. Eng.* SE-2, no. 4 (December 1976): 265-273.
3. B. Lientz, E. Swanson, and G. Tompkins, "Characteristics of Application Software Maintenance," *CACM* 21, no. 6 (June 1978): 466-471.
4. B. Boehm, J. Brown, H. Kaspar, M. Lipow, G. MacLeod, and M. Merrit, *Characteristics of Software Quality* (New York: North-Holland Publishing, 1978): 2-1.
5. M. Zelkowitz, *Principles of Software Engineering and Design* (Englewood Cliffs, NJ: Prentice-Hall, 1979): 2-11.
6. B. Boehm, J. Brown, and M. Lipow, "Quantitative Evaluation of Software Quality," in *2nd International Conference on Software Engineering Proc.* (San Francisco), October 13-15, 1976, pp. 592-605.
7. B. Boehm, "Quantitative Evaluation of Software Qualtiy," pp. 595-605.
8. C. McClure, "Formalization and Application of Structured Programming and Program Complexity," (Ph.D. thesis, Illinois Institute of Technology, May 1976), pp. 57-100.
9. B. Boehm, "Quantitative Evaluation of Software Quality," p. 600.
10. B. Boehm, H. Kaspar, M. Lipow, G. MacLeod and M. Merrit, *Characteristics of Software Quality*, pp. 3-1-3-26.
11. D. Gelperin, "Testing Maintainability," *ACM SIGSOFT Software Engineering Notes*, 4, no. 2 (April 1979): 7-12.
12. B. Boehm, "Seven Basic Principles of Software Engineering," in *Infotech State of the Art Reports: Software Engineering Techniques* (Maidenhead, England: Infotech International, 1977): 77-113.
13. P. Wegner, "Research Directions in Software Technology," in *3rd International Conference on Software Engineering Proc.* (Atlanta), May 10-12, 1978, pp. 243-259.
14. M. Zelkowitz, *Principles of Software Engineering and Design*, pp. 2-11.
15. M. Zelkowitz, *Principles of Software Engineering and Design*, pp. 2-11.
16. B. Boehm, R. McClean, and D. Urfrig, "Some Experiences with Automated Aids to the Design of Large-Scale Reliable Software," *IEEE Trans. on Soft. Eng.*, SE-1, no. 1 (March 1975): 125-133.
17. M. Zelkowitz, "Perspectives on Software Engineering," *Computing Surveys*, 10, no. 2 (June 1978): 197-216.
18. C. McClure, *Reducing Cobol Complexity through Structured Programming*, (New York, NY: Van Nostrand Reinhold, 1978): 43-76.

19. M. Zelkowitz, *Principles of Software Engineering and Design*, pp. 2–11.
20. D. Gelperin, "Testing Maintainability," pp. 7–12.
21. D. Parnas, "Designing for Ease of Extension and Contraction," *IEEE Trans. on Soft. Eng.*, SE-5, no. 2 (March 1979): 128–137.
22. D. Parnas, "Designing for Ease of Extension and Contraction," pp. 128–137.
23. D. Parnas, "Designing for Ease of Extension and Contraction," pp. 128–137.
24. B. Boehm, "Seven Basic Principles of Software Engineering, pp. 77–113.
25. C. McClure, *Reducing COBOL Complexity*, pp. 1–7.
26. C. McClure, *Reducing COBOL Complexity*, pp. 1–7.
27. G. Myers, "A Controlled Experiment in Program Testing and Code Walkthroughs/Inspections," *CACM*, 21, no. 9 (September 1978): 760–768.
28. J. Elshoff, "An Analysis of Some Commercial PL/1 Programs," *IEEE Trans. on Software Eng.*, SE-2, no. 2 (June 1976): 113–120.
29. *Structured Programming Guide*, IBM FSC (1974).
30. T. McCabe, "A Complexity Measure," *IEEE Trans. on Soft. Eng.*, SE-2, no. 4 (December 1976): 308–320.
31. C. McClure, "A Model for Program Complexity Analysis," in *3rd International Conference on Software Engineering Proc.* (Atlanta), May 10–12, 1978, pp. 149–157.
32. D. Van Tassel, *Program Style, Design, Efficiency, Debugging and Testing*, (Englewood Cliffs, NJ: Prentice-Hall, 1979): 238–284.
33. D. Van Tassel, *Program Style, Design, Efficiency, Debugging and Testing*, pp. 238–284.
34. H. Mills, "Software Development," pp. 265–273.
35. G. Myers, "A Controlled Experiment in Program Testing and Code Walkthroughs/Inspections," pp. 760–768.

Chapter 4

1. G. Weinberg, *The Psychology of Computer Programming*, (New York, New York: Van Nostrand Reinhold, 1971): 67–94.
2. G. Weinberg, *The Psychology of Computer Programming*, pp. 47–66.
3. F. Baker and H. Mills, "Chief Programmer Teams," *IBM Systems Journal* 11 no. 1 (1972): 56–73.
4. A. Hoare, "Keynote Address: Software Engineering," in the *3rd International Conference on Software Engineering Proc.* (Atlanta), May 10–12, 1978, pp. 1–4.
5. F. Brooks, *The Mythical Man-Month*, (Reading, Mass.: Addison-Wesley Publishing Co., 1975): 29–37.

Chapter 5

1. W. Myers, "The Social Implications of Computers," *Computer*, 12, no. 8 (August, 1979): 79–86.

2. D. Reifer, "Controlling," *Tutorial: Software Management*, IEEE Catalog No. EHO 146-1, p. 205.
3. "Structured Walk-Throughs," in *Improved Programming Technologies Management Overview*, IBM Data Processing Division Systems Marketing Installation Productivity Programs Dept., August, 1973.

Chapter 6

1. B. Lientz, E. Swanson and G. Tompkins, "Characteristics of Application Software Maintenance," *CACM* 21, no. 6 (June 1978): 466–471.
2. F. Brooks, *The Mythical Man-Month* (Reading, Mass.: Addison-Wesley Publishing Co.), 1975, pp. 121-123.
3. S. Yau and J. Collofello, "Some Stability Measures for Software Maintenance," in *IEEE 3rd International Computer Software and Application Conference Proc.* (Chicago), Nov. 6-8, 1979, pp. 674-679.
4. Lientz, Swanson and Tompkins, "Characteristics of Application Software Maintenance," pp. 466–471.
5. J. Munson, "Software Maintainability: A practical Concern for Life-Cycle Costs," in *IEEE 2nd International Computer Software and Application Conference Proc.* (Chicago), Nov. 13-16, 1978, pp. 54-59.
6. Lientz, Swanson and Tompkins, "Characteristics of Application Software Maintenance," pp. 466–471.
7. B. Boehm, "Seven Basic Principles of Software Engineering," in *Infotech State of the Art Reports: Software Engineering Techniques* (Maidenhead, England: Infotech International, 1977): 77-113.
8. Boehm, "Seven Basic Principles of Software Engineering," pp. 77-113.
9. W. Myers, "A Statistical Approach to Scheduling Software Development," *Computer* 11, no. 12 (December 1978), 23-35.
10. M. Zelkowitz, *Principles of Software Engineering and Design* (Englewood Cliffs, NJ: Prentice-Hall, 1979): 12-24.
11. Zelkowitz, *Principles of Software Engineering and Design,* pp. 12-24.
12. Myers, "A Statistical Approach to Scheduling Software Development," pp. 23-35.
13. Zelkowitz, *Principles of Software Engineering and Design*, pp. 12-24.
14. Zelkowitz, *Principles of Software Engineering and Design*, pp. 12-24.
15. Myers, "A Statistical Approach to Scheduling Software Development," pp. 23-35.
16. Myers, "A Statistical Approach to Scheduling Software Development," pp. 23-35.
17. Myers, "A Statistical Approach to Scheduling Software Development," pp. 23-35.
18. H. Mills, "Software Development," *IEEE Trans. on Soft. Eng.* SE-2, no. 4 (December 1976): 265-273.
19. S. Yau, J. Collofello and T. MacGregor, "Ripple Effect Analysis on Software Maintenance," in *IEEE 2nd International Computer Software and*

Application Conference Proc. (Chicago) November 13-16, 1978, pp. 60-65.
20. E. Swanson, "The Dimensions of Maintenance," in *IEEE 2nd International Conference on Software Engineering Proc.* (San Francisco) October 13-15, 1976, pp. 492-497.
21. Lientz, Swanson and Tompkins, "Characteristics of Application Software Maintenance," pp. 466-471.
22. Yau, Collofello and MacGregor, "Ripple Effect Analysis on Software Maintenance," pp. 60-65.

Chapter 7

1. B. Lientz, E. Swanson and G. Tompkins, "Characteristics of Application Software Maintenance," *CACM* 21, no. 6 (June 1978): 466-471.
2. F. Brooks, *The Mythical Man-Month* (Reading, Mass.: Addison-Wesley Publishing Co.), 1975, pp. 32-35.
3. Lientz, Swanson and Tompkins, "Characteristics of Application Software Maintenance," pp. 466-471.
4. Lientz, Swanson and Tompkins, "Charcteristics of Application Software Maintenance," pp. 466-471.
5. Lientz, Swanson and Tompkins, "Characteristics of Application Software Maintenance," pp. 466-471.
6. E. Swanson, "The Dimensions of Maintenance," in *IEEE 2nd International Conference on Software Engineering Proc.* (San Francisco) October 13-15, 1976, pp. 492-497.
7. D. Parnas, "Designing for Ease of Extension and Contraction," *IEEE Trans of Soft. Eng.* SE-5, no. 2 (March 1979): 128-137.
8. W. Cabe and A. Salisbury, "Controlling the Software Life Cycle-The Project Management Task," *IEEE Trans. on Soft. Eng.* SE-4, no 4 (July 1978): 326-334.
9. Brooks, *The Mythical Man-Month*, pp. 121-123.

Chapter 8

1. B. Boehm, "Seven Basic Principles of Software Engineering," in *Infotech State of the Art Reports: Software Engineering Techniques* (Maidenhead, England: Infotech International, 1977): 77-113.

Bibliography

Baker, F. and Mills, H. "Chief Programmer Teams." *IBM Systems Journal* 11 no. 1 (1972): 56-73.
Basili, V. and Zelkowitz, M. "Analyzing Medium-Scale Software Development." *3rd International Conference on Software Engineering*, May 1978, pp. 116-123.
Boehm, B. "Software and Its Impact: A Quantitative Assessment." *Datamation* 19 no. 5 (May 1973): 48-59.
Boehm, B., McClean, R. and Urfrig, D. "Some Experiences with Automated Aids to the Design of Large Scale Reliable Software," *IEEE Trans. on Software Engineering* SE-1 no. 1 (March 1975): 125-133.
Boehm, B., Brown, J. and Lipow, M. "Quantitative Evaluation of Software Quality." *2nd International Conference on Software Engineering*, October 1976, pp. 592-605.
Boehm, B. "Seven Basic Principles of Software Engineering," in *Infotech State of the Art Reports: Software Engineering Techniques*. Maidenhead, England: Infotech International, 1977.
Boehm, B., Brown, J., Kaspar, H., Lipow, M., MacLeod, G. and Merrit, M. *Characteristics of Software Quality*. New York: North-Holland, 1978.
Brooks, F. *The Mythical Man-Month*. Reading, Mass.: Addison Wesley Publishing Co., 1975.
Cave, W. and Salisbury, A. "Controlling the Software Life Cycle—The Project Management Task." *IEEE Trans. on Software Engineering* (July 1978): 326-334.
Cooper, J. "Corporate Level Software Management." *IEEE Trans. on Software Engineering* SE-4 no. 4 (July 1978): 319-326.
Curtis, B., Sheppard, S., Milliman, P., Borst, M. and Love, T. "Measuring the Psychological Complexity of Software Maintenance Tasks with Halsted and McCabe Metrics." *IEEE Trans. on Software Engineering* SE-5 no. 2 (March 1979): 96-104.
DeRoze, B. and Nyman, T. "The Software Life Cycle—A Management and Technological Challenge in the Department of Defense." *IEEE Trans. on Software Engineering* SE-4 no. 4 (July 1978): 309-318.

DeYoung, G. and Kampen, G. "Program Factors as Predictors of Program Readability." *3rd International Computer Software and Application Conference*, Nov. 1979. pp. 668–673.

Elshoff, J. "An Analysis of Some Commercial PL/1 Programs." *IEEE Trans. on Software Engineering* SE-2 no. 2 (June 1976): 113–120.

Gelperin, D. "Testing Maintainability." *ACM SIGSOFT Software Engineering Notes* 4 no. 2 (April 1979): 7–12.

Gilb, T. "A Comment on The Definition of Maintainability." *ACM SIGSOFT Software Engineering Notes* 4 no. 3 (July 1979): 32–33.

Hamilton, K. and Block, A. "Programmer Productivity in a Structured Environment," *Infosystems* (April 1979): 44–50.

Hetzel, B. "A Perspective on Software Development." *3rd International Conference on Software Engineering*, May 1978, pp. 260–263.

Hoare, C. "Software Engineering: A Keynote Address." *3rd International Conference on Software Engineering*, May 1978, pp. 1–4.

"IBM Federal System Center Structured Programming Guide." IBM FSC, 1974.

Jensen, R. and Tonies, C. *Software Engineering.* Englewood Cliffs, N.J.: Prentice-Hall, 1978.

Knight, B. "On Software Quality and Productivity," in *Technical Directions*. IBM FSC (July 1978): 21–27.

Lientz, B., Swanson, E. and Tompkins, G. "Characteristics of Application Software Maintenance." *CACM* 21 no. 6 (June 1978): 466–471.

Litecky, C. and Davis, G. "A Study of Errors, Error-Proneness and Error Diagnosis in COBOL." *CACM* 19 no. 1 (January 1976): 33–37.

Liu, C. "A Look at Software Maintenance." *Datamation* 22 no. 11 (November 1976): 51–55.

McCabe, T. "A Complexity Measure," *IEEE Trans. on Software Engineering* SE-2 no. 4 (December 1976): 308–320.

McCammon, S. "Applied Software Engineering: A Real-Time Simulator Case History." *IEEE Trans. on Software Engineering* SE-1 no. 4 (December 1975): 377–383.

McClure, C. "A Model for Program Complexity Analysis." *3rd International Conference on Software Engineering.* May 1978, pp. 149–157.

McClure, C. *Reducing COBOL Complexity through Structured Programming.* New York: Van Nostrand Reinhold, 1978.

McHenry, R. and Walston, C. "Software Life Cycle Management: Weapons Process Developer." *IEEE Trans. on Software Engineering* SE-4 no. 4 (July 1978): 334–344.

Metzger, P. *Managing a Programming Project.* Englewood Cliffs, NJ: Prentice-Hall, 1973.

Miller, E. et al. "Workshop Report: Software Testing and Test Documentation." *Computer* 12 no. 3 (March 1979): 98–107.

Miller, L. "Harlan Mills on the Psychology of Quality," *IBM Research Center* RC 3779 Reissue No. 19598 (May 31, 1973).

Mills, H. "Software Development." *IEEE Trans. on Software Engineering* SE-2 no. 4 (December 1976): 265–273.

Munson, J. "Software Maintainability: A Practical Concern for Life Cycle Costs." *2nd International Computer Software and Application Conference*, Nov. 1978, pp. 54–59.

Myers, G. "A Controlled Experiment in Program Testing and Code Walkthroughs/Inspections." *CACM* 21 no. 9 (September 1978): 760–768.

Myers, W. "The Social Implications of Computers." *Computer* 12 no. 8 (August 1979): 79–86.

Parnas, D. "Designing for Ease of Extension and Contraction," *IEEE Trans. on Software Engineering* SE-5 no. 2 (March 1979): 128–137.

Raduchel, W. "Managing Software Development." *ACM SIGSOFT Software Engineering Notes* 3 no. 4 (October 1978): 22–26.

Reifer, D. "Controlling." *Tutorial: Software Management* IEEE Catalog No. EHO 146-1, p. 205.

Scott, R. and Simmons, D. "Predicting Programming Group Productivity—A Communications Model," *IEEE Trans. on Software Engineering* SE-1 no. 4 (December 1975): 411–414.

Strong, E. "Software Reliability and Maintainability in Large-Scale Systems." *2nd International Computer Software and Application Conference*, Nov. 1978, pp. 755–759.

"Structured Walk-Throughs," in *Improved Programming Technologies Management Overview*, IBM Data Processing Division Systems Marketing Installation Productivity Programs Dept. (August 1973).

Swanson, E. "The Dimensions of Maintenance," *2nd International Conference on Software Engineering*, Oct. 1976, pp. 492–497.

Turn, R. Davis, M. and Reinstedt. "A Management Approach to the Development of Computer-Based Systems." *2nd International Conference on Software Engineering*, Oct. 1976, pp. 305–311.

Van Tassel, D. *Program Style, Design, Efficiency, Debugging and Testing*. Englewood Cliffs, NJ: Prentice-Hall, 1979.

Wasserman, A. "Panel on Problems of the 80's." *3rd International Conference on Software Engineering*, May 1978, p. 341.

Wegner, P. "Research Directions in Software Technology," *3rd International Conference on Software Engineering*, May 1978, pp. 243–259.

Weinberg, G. *Psychology of Computer Programming*. New York: Van Nostrand Reinhold, 1971.

Yau, S., Collofello, J. and MacGregor, T. "Ripple Effect Analysis on Software Maintenance." *2nd International Computer Software and Application Conference*, Nov. 1978, pp. 60–65.

Yau, S. and Collofello, J. "Some Stability Measures for Software Maintenance." *3rd International Computer Software and Application Conference*, Nov. 1979, pp. 466–471.

Zelkowitz, M. "Perspectives on Software Engineering." *Computing Surveys* 10 no. 2 (June 1978): 297–316.

Zelkowitz, M. *Principles of Software Engineering and Design*. Englewood Cliffs, NJ.: Prentice-Hall, 1979.

Index

acceptance reviews. *See* reviews
audits, 39-40, 56, 81, 108, 135, 140-141, 165. *See also* software audits
automated tools, 5

backup programmer, 75-79, 81, 84. *See also* chief programmer team
Boehm, 35-36
bottom-up design, 5, 11-12, 17-18, 20, 23, 46-49

check-point reviews, 99, 101, 108-109, 111-116, 123, 125, 143, 153, 160-162, 167. *See also* reviews
chief programmer, 75-82, 86, 88. *See also* chief programmer team
chief programmer team, 2, 14-15, 18-19, 21, 72, 74-82, 86-91
coding phase, 32, 34, 52-58, 67, 69, 112, 126. *See also* software life cycle
complexity, 41, 56-58, 68-70, 108, 135, 137, 140, 147, 156-157, 160-161, 169
Complexity Profile, 58, 68, 147-148, 157-158, 168
co-pilot, 79-81. *See also* surgical team
CPT. *See* chief programmer team

data processing, 3, 29, 70, 78-79, 88, 91
design phase, 16, 20, 23, 25, 32, 34, 44-52, 67, 69, 72, 88, 96-97, 111, 150, 153, 161. *See also* software life cycle
documentation, 30, 39, 53, 55, 67, 88, 108, 113, 136-137, 140, 160

Egoless programming, 72-78, 82, 85, 90

freeze-points, 109, 113-114, 117, 126-127. *See also* reviews

hardest-first strategy, 16, 18. *See also* design phase
Hoare, 77

introduction reviews, 99, 114, 116, 119, 123, 125, 143, 167. *See also* reviews

language lawyer, 80. *See also* surgical team

maintainability. *See* software maintainability
maintenance. *See* software maintenance
Maintenance Support Plan, 144, 161
milestones. *See* check-point reviews
Myers, 56, 65

operation and maintenance phase, 29, 32, 40, 42, 44, 87. *See also* software maintenance

phase chief, 96-98, 108, 114, 117, 120-122, 126-127, 130. *See also* revised chief programmer team
portability. *See* software portability
program complexity, 20-21. *See also* complexity
programmer productivity, 2-3, 19-20, 22, 53-54, 72, 145-146, 169. *See also* software effort estimates
programming, 1, 52, 70-71, 77, 145
programming secretary, 76, 79. *See also* chief programmer team
project co-leader, 82-84, 87-91, 108, 167, 172. *See also* revised chief programmer team

201

INDEX

project control documents, 123–124, 190
project leader, 82–91, 94, 96, 98, 108, 120, 122, 128, 130, 167, 188–190. *See also* revised chief programmer team
project management, 6–13, 25–26, 55, 70–71, 74, 81, 86, 91–93, 99, 120, 140, 163
project status reporting, 117, 120–123, 130

RCPT. *See* revised chief programmer team
requirements analysis, 5, 16, 25, 32, 40–43, 48, 50, 66, 68, 150, 152, 161. *See also* software life cycle
revalidation, 157–162
reviews, 37, 39, 43, 50, 55, 93, 99, 140, 150
revised chief programmer team, 81–91, 94, 96, 130, 166–167, 180
ripple effect, 148, 150, 154–157, 161

Shooman, 45
software, 1–4, 31–34, 39, 70–71, 75, 78, 81, 108, 126, 130, 133–136, 139, 146, 171, 185–190
software audits, 37. *See also* audits
software change, 30, 42, 51, 65, 68–69, 93, 108, 125–130, 133–136, 139, 147–148, 150, 152, 154–157, 160–164, 168, 171, 174–182, 188
software change control, 121–130, 174–182
software complexity. *See* complexity
Software Crisis, 1
software development, 1–10, 20, 22, 26, 29–31, 34, 37–41, 43–45, 48, 65, 68, 70, 72–75, 81–82, 92, 95–96, 100, 108–109, 114, 126, 130, 133, 143–144, 189–190
software development team, 2, 9, 13, 26, 30, 70–74, 78, 88, 93, 114, 117, 126, 128, 140, 164, 168, 172, 180–182, 188–190
software efficiency, 36–37, 152, 154, 188
software effort estimates, 9, 10, 144–148, 169, 171
software engineering, 1–13, 20–26, 29, 34, 40, 72, 77, 93, 133–135, 138–139, 141, 143, 146, 160, 185–186, 190

software errors, 30, 45, 63–64, 68–69, 73, 126, 133–134, 136, 147, 157–158, 160, 168–169, 175
software life cycle, 2, 4–5, 29–34, 39, 42, 52, 83, 123, 133, 150, 163–165, 171, 175–176, 179–180, 186–190
software maintainability, 36–40, 51–57, 65, 68, 72, 88, 135, 138, 143, 159, 163, 167, 172, 188–189
software maintainer, 37, 40, 42, 44, 50–52, 63, 65, 68–69, 72, 87, 93, 108, 114, 130, 135, 138–139, 143, 147, 160–161, 186–190
software maintenance, 2–5, 23, 26, 29–31, 39, 52–54, 63, 68, 126, 133–145, 148, 150–182, 189–190
software maintenance team, 165–174, 180–182
software modifiability, 36
software modification, 150–157, 160–162, 175–176. *See also* software change
software portability, 36–37
software readability, 53, 56–57, 69, 73–74. *See also* software understandability
software reliability, 36, 43, 45, 52–53, 63, 65, 74, 88, 133, 152, 188
software testability, 36, 57
software understandability, 23, 36, 56–57, 188. *See also* software readability
software usability, 36, 40, 57, 72, 88, 160, 175, 188
software user, 39–44, 49–52, 55, 72, 77, 82, 86, 88, 93, 114, 120, 126, 130, 134–136, 139, 152–154, 158, 160, 163, 170, 175–177, 182, 185–186, 188–190
software product. *See* software
software project, 1, 4, 7–10, 26, 92, 99, 130, 185
software quality, 30–31, 34–37, 40, 68, 87–88, 99, 108, 117, 130, 133, 135, 137, 140–141, 150, 152–155, 159–162, 168–171, 176, 188–189
software redevelopment, 136–138
software standards, 37, 39, 44, 55–56, 65–68, 72, 74, 77, 99, 108, 117, 140–141, 147, 154, 188
software system, 2, 4, 6, 23, 30, 37, 40–41, 46, 48, 51, 56, 65, 72, 74. *See also* software

specification phase, 32, 42-45, 48, 50, 67-68, 110, 114, 126, 150-153, 161. *See also* software life cycle
structured design, 46. *See also* design phase
structured programming, 1-7, 20, 23, 34, 43, 52-55, 57, 68, 154
structured walk-through, 99-101, 108, 112, 117, 130
surgeon, 79-81, 86. *See also* surgical team
surgical team, 79-82, 85, 90-91
system. *See* software system
system support. *See* software maintenance
System Development Journal, 39, 67, 99, 125, 130, 140, 147, 168-169, 189
System Maintenance Journal, 141, 154, 178, 190

Test History, 63-64, 68, 147, 149, 157-159, 168, 190
test plan, 5, 19, 23, 25, 63, 65, 74, 88
tester, 80. *See also* surgical team
testing, 18-21, 32, 34, 53, 58-65, 68-69, 113, 127, 133, 157, 162. *See also* software life cycle
  acceptance testing, 59, 62-64, 69, 157-158, 162
  integration testing, 18, 59-62, 64, 69, 157-158, 162
  system testing, 18-19, 59, 62, 64, 69, 157-158, 162
  unit testing, 18-19, 59-60, 64, 69, 73, 157-158, 162
toolsmith, 80. *See also* surgical team
top-down design, 2, 5, 11-12, 15-16, 18, 20, 23, 34, 46-49

user liaison, 82-91, 108, 128, 167-168, 170, 172, 178-182, 188. *See also* revised chief programmer team
Weinberg, 35, 71